TEACHER'S PET PUBLICATIONS

LITPLAN TEACHER PACK
for
Island of the Blue Dolphins
based on the book by
Scott O'Dell

Written by
Janine H. Sherman

© 1996 Teacher's Pet Publications
All Rights Reserved

This **LitPlan** for Scott O'Dell's
Island of the Blue Dolphins
has been brought to you by Teacher's Pet Publications, Inc.

Copyright Teacher's Pet Publications 1996
11504 Hammock Point
Berlin MD 21811

Only the student materials in this unit plan (such as worksheets,
study questions, and tests) may be reproduced multiple times
for use in the purchaser's classroom.

For any additional copyright questions,
contact Teacher's Pet Publications.

www.tpet.com

TABLE OF CONTENTS - *Island of the Blue Dolphins*

Introduction	5
Unit Objectives	8
Reading Assignment Sheet	9
Unit Outline	10
Study Questions (Short Answer)	13
Quiz/Study Questions (Multiple Choice)	28
Pre-reading Vocabulary Worksheets	51
Lesson One (Introductory Lesson)	65
Nonfiction Assignment Sheet	96
Oral Reading Evaluation Form	86
Writing Assignment 1	68
Writing Assignment 2	74
Writing Assignment 3	95
Writing Evaluation Form	79
Vocabulary Review Activities	98
Extra Writing Assignments/Discussion ?s	88
Unit Review Activities	100
Unit Tests	103
Unit Resource Materials	143
Vocabulary Resource Materials	161

A FEW NOTES ABOUT THE AUTHOR
Scott O'Dell

O'DELL, Scott (1898-1989). Scott O'Dell was born on Terminal Island, a part of Los Angeles, California, on May 23, 1898. He claims L.A. was a frontier town then with more horses than automobiles and more jackrabbits than people. The very first sound he can remember was a wildcat scratching on the roof while he lay in bed. His father was a railroad man, so Scott moved around a lot as a child. Many of the places he lived show up as settings for his stories. He attended four different colleges and universities. He worked as a motion picture technical director and cameraman before becoming a newspaperman and an author.

Many of O'Dell's books are set in the past, but the issues dealt with are timeless. He felt writing historical fiction for children was very important work because according to him, "No educated person can live a complete life without a knowledge of where we came from." He claims he was didactic- he wanted to teach through his books. He says, "History has a direct bearing on children's lives."

His best known book is the Newbery Medal, *Island of the Blue Dolphins* (1961). While researching the history of California, O'Dell discovered an article about the Lost Woman of San Nicolas. This provided the inspiration for *Island of the Blue Dolphins*. It takes place on some islands that are much like those he lived on as a kid. He put many of his happy childhood memories in it: the look of the islands, the colors and sounds of the sea, and the wild creatures that lived there. He also wrote the book in anger at the hunters who invaded the mountains where he lived and slaughtered everything that crept or flew. This anger was also directed against himself, who at a young age, committed the same crimes against nature.

O'Dell felt that writing for children was more rewarding than writing for adults. He knew that if children like your book they respond for a long time with thousands of letters. It was this response that made the task of writing worth doing for this author. During his lifetime, Scott O'Dell received more than 2,000 letters a year from his young readers. When Scott wasn't writing, he liked to read and to work in the sun; gardening, planting trees, and fishing.

O'Dell published over two dozen books for children including: *The King's Fifth* (1967), *The Black Pearl* (1968), *Sing Down the Moon* (1971), *Zia* (1976), and *Black Star, Bright Dawn* (1988).

INTRODUCTION - *Island of the Blue Dolphins*

This unit has been designed to develop students' reading, writing, thinking, and language skills through exercises and activities related to *Island of the Blue Dolphins* by Scott O'Dell. It includes twenty lessons supported by extra resource materials.

The **introductory lesson** introduces students to the factual basis of the novel discovered by Scott O'Dell. Following the introductory activity, students are given the materials they will be using during the unit.

The **reading assignments** are approximately twenty pages each; some are a little shorter while others are a little longer. Students have approximately 15 minutes of Pre-reading work to do prior to each reading assignment. This Pre-reading work involves reviewing the study questions for the assignment and doing some vocabulary work for ten or less vocabulary words they will encounter in their reading.

The **study guide questions** are fact-based questions; students can find the answers to these questions right in the text. These questions come in two formats: short answer or multiple choice. The best use of these materials is probably to use the short answer version of the questions as study guides for students (since answers will be more complete), and to use the multiple choice version for occasional quizzes. It might be a good idea to make transparencies of your answer keys for the overhead projector.

The **vocabulary work** is intended to enrich students' vocabularies as well as to aid in the students' understanding of the book. Prior to each reading assignment, students will complete a two-part worksheet for approximately ten or less vocabulary words in the upcoming reading assignment. Part I focuses on students' use of general knowledge and contextual clues by giving the sentence in which the word appears in the text. Students are then to write down what they think the words mean based on the words' usage. Part II nails down the definitions of the words by giving students dictionary definitions of the words and having students match the words to the correct definitions based on the words' contextual usage. Students should then have an understanding of the words when they meet them in the text.

After each reading assignment, students will go back and formulate answers for the study guide questions. Discussion of these questions serves as a **review** of the most important events and ideas presented in the reading assignments.

After students complete extra discussion questions, there is a **vocabulary review** lesson which pulls together all of the fragmented vocabulary lists for the reading assignments and gives students a review of all of the words they have studied.

Following the reading of the book, two lessons are devoted to the **extra discussion questions/writing assignments/activities** . These questions focus on interpretation, critical analysis and personal response, employing a variety of thinking skills and adding to the students' understanding of the novel. These questions are done as a **group activity**. Using the information they have acquired so far through individual work and class discussions, students get together to further examine the text and to brainstorm ideas relating to the themes of the novel.

The group activity is followed by two **reports and discussion/ activity** sessions in which the groups share their ideas about the book with the entire class; thus, the entire class gets exposed to many different ideas regarding the themes and events of the book.

There are three **writing assignments** in this unit, each with the purpose of informing, persuading, or having students express personal opinions. The first assignment gives students the opportunity to express personal opinion: students will keep a diary throughout the reading of the novel. The second assignment gives students the chance to persuade: students are to select their ideal vacation location and convince their parents it's the spot for the next family vacation. The third assignment is to inform: students select a topic of interest to them from the Extra Activities or More Activities section in Unit Resource Materials to research and summarize in a composition.

In addition, there is a **nonfiction reading assignment.** Students are required to read a piece of nonfiction related in some way to *Island of the Blue Dolphins*. In this case, it ties in with their Writing Assignment #3. After reading their nonfiction pieces, students will fill out a worksheet on which they answer questions regarding facts, interpretation, criticism, and personal opinions. During one class period, students make **oral presentations** about the nonfiction pieces they have read. This not only exposes all students to a wealth of information, it also gives students the opportunity to practice **public speaking**.

Writing Assignment #2 is followed by a **project** which students complete independently, outside of class. Students are to create a travel poster and brochure advertising their chosen vacation spot. Sharing of these will be done as part of the **reports and discussion / activity** sessions held at the end of the unit.

The **review lesson** pulls together all of the aspects of the unit. The teacher is given four or five choices of activities or games to use which all serve the same basic function of reviewing all of the information presented in the unit.

The **unit test** comes in two formats: all multiple choice-matching-true/false or with a mixture of matching, short answer, and composition. As a convenience, two different tests for each format have been included.

There are additional **support materials** included with this unit. The **extra activities packet** includes suggestions for an in-class library, crossword and word search puzzles related to the novel, and extra vocabulary worksheets. There is a list of **bulletin board ideas** which gives the teacher suggestions for bulletin boards to go along with this unit. In addition, there is a list of **extra class activities** the teacher could choose from to enhance the unit or as a substitution for an exercise the teacher might feel is inappropriate for his/her class. **Answer keys** are located directly after the **reproducible student materials** throughout the unit. The student materials may be reproduced for use in the teacher's classroom without infringement of copyrights. No other portion of this unit may be reproduced without the written consent of Teacher's Pet Publications, Inc.

UNIT OBJECTIVES *Island of the Blue Dolphins*

1. Through reading Scott O'Dell's *Island of the Blue Dolphins,* students will gain an appreciation of the need for companionship.

2. Students will determine traits necessary for survival.

3. Students will do research to become familiar with relevant physical, geographical, and cultural aspects of a Californian coastal island and its inhabitants.

4. Students will become familiar with and able to identify various forms of sea life and plants.

5. Students will demonstrate their understanding of the text on four levels: factual, interpretive, critical and personal.

6. Students will gain appreciation for and demonstrate proficiency in identifying and using figurative language.

7. Students will be given the opportunity to practice reading aloud and silently to improve their skills in each area.

8. Students will answer questions to demonstrate their knowledge and understanding of the main events and characters in *Island of the Blue Dolphins* as they relate to the author's theme development.

9. Students will enrich their vocabularies and improve their understanding of the novel through the vocabulary lessons prepared for use in conjunction with the novel.

10. The writing assignments in this unit are geared to several purposes:
    a. To have students demonstrate their abilities to inform, to persuade, or to express their own personal ideas
    > Note: Students will demonstrate ability to write effectively to <u>inform</u> by developing and organizing facts to convey information. Students will demonstrate the ability to write effectively to <u>persuade</u> by selecting and organizing relevant information, establishing an argumentative purpose, and by designing an appropriate strategy for an identified audience. Students will demonstrate the ability to write effectively to <u>express personal ideas</u> by selecting a form and its appropriate elements.

    b. To check the students' reading comprehension
    c. To make students think about the ideas presented by the novel

READING ASSIGNMENT SHEET - *Island of the Blue Dolphins*

Date to be Assigned	Chapters	Completion Date
	Author's Note pp. 182-184 Chapters 1-3	
	Chapters 4-7	
	Chapters 8, 9	
	Chapters 10-12	
	Chapters 13-15	
	Chapters 16-18	
	Chapters 19-21	
	Chapters 22-25	
	Chapters 26-29	

UNIT OUTLINE - *Island of the Blue Dolphins*

1	2	3	4	5
Introduction Author's Note PVR Ch. 1-3	Study ? Ch. 1-3 Writing Assignment #1 PVR Ch. 4-7	Study ? Ch. 4-7 Conflict PVR Ch. 8,9	Study ? Ch. 8, 9 Prediction PVR Ch. 10-12	Study ? Ch. 10-12 Decision-making
6	7	8	9	10
PVR Ch. 13-15 Writing Assignment #2 Project	Study ? Ch. 13-15 PVR Ch. 16-18	Study ? Ch. 16-18 Survival	PVR Ch. 19-21 Writing Conference	Figurative Language
13	12	13	14	15
Study? Ch. 19-21 Companionship PVR Ch. 22-25	Study ?Ch. 22-25 PVR Ch. 26-29 Oral Reading Evaluation	Extra Discussion Questions	Extra Discussion Questions/ Activities	Writing Assignment #3
16	17	18	19	20
Project/Writing Assignment #2 Sharing	Nonfiction Reading Oral Presentation	Vocabulary Review	Review	Test

Key: P=Preview Study Questions   V= Vocabulary Work   R= Read

STUDY GUIDE QUESTIONS

SHORT ANSWER STUDY GUIDE QUESTIONS - *Island of the Blue Dolphins*

Author's Note, Chapters 1-3
1. How and when was the island in this story actually discovered by white men?
2. Whose true story is this novel based upon?
3. Where is she buried and where was her cormorant skirt sent?
4. How many miles from Los Angeles is San Nicholas?
5. For what is the island used today?
6. What were Ramo and Karana doing when the Aleut ship came?
7. Describe the men rowing the small boat to shore from the ship.
8. For what reason had the Russian and his crew come to the island?
9. What agreement of payment was reached between the Aleuts and the Chief?
10. Why do the islanders have a secret name?
11. Describe the Island of the Blue Dolphins.
12. What does Chief Chowig order concerning his tribe and the Aleuts?
13. What good fortune befalls the islanders that spring?
14. Give a description of the men who come to ask for fish. Tell the Chief's response.
15. Describe the sea otters.
16. Explain the otter slaughtering process as told by Karana.
17. Why were tribesmen sent to hollow out a log in the cove and sleep beside it at night?
18. Share three observations made by the islanders that indicate the visitors prepare to leave soon.
19. What is Karana's father doing at the end of the chapter that leads you to believe he does not trust the agreement?

Chapters 4-7
1. Why did the tribe hurry to Coral Cove on the sunless day?
2. How many bales of otter pelts had the hunters bundled?
3. What does Chief Chowig agree to do after the other chests are delivered from the ship?
4. Describe the battle between the hunters and the island warriors.
5. What do his daughters and the village say weakened Chief Chowig?
6. How many warriors were killed in the battle?
7. Why did the village wait three days to bury the dead?
8. What was done with the dead Aleuts?
9. Who was named the new chief and why?
10. How does life change in Ghalas-at?
11. What was Ulape and Karana's job?
12. Why does Kimki leave the island?
13. What is the tribe's plan, under Matasaip's leadership, if the Aleuts return?

Short Answer Study Guide Questions - *Island of the Blue Dolphins* Page 2

Chapters 4-7 Continued
14. Nanko brings what news?
15. How does Ulape, readying for the voyage, indicate she is unmarried?
16. Why had Ramo missed the boat?
17. What does Karana do when she realizes the ship is not returning for her brother?

Chapters 8, 9
1. Where does Ramo go alone against Karana's instructions?
2. What happens to him?
3. After this happens to him, what does Karana vow?
4. How does Karana end the haunting village's sights and sounds?
5. Why does she search for weapons that may have been left behind?
6. What is she looking for in the chest left by the Aleuts? What does she find?
7. Karana fears bad things may happen to her. Why?
8. What makes her decide to go against the tribe's law?
9. Why is it difficult for her to make the weapons?
10. How does she make her rock bed on the headland more comfortable?

Chapters 10-12
1. Why is Karana losing hope of a ship returning?
2. What decision has Karana made during the storm?
3. How does she feel about her decision?
4. What lessens her fears while on the sea at night?
5. What problem develops and how does she solve it?
6. Why does she decide to turn back for the island?
7. How do the dolphins influence Karana?
8. In what way do Karana's feelings change when she returns to the island?
9. What does she decide she must do first? What requirements are there?
10. Out of what does Karana build a fence?
11. Describe the house she builds.
12. How is Karana able to work at night with no sunlight?
13. What does Karana require for her spear?

Chapters 13-15
1. Describe the cow, bull, and sea elephants.
2. What warning of her father's enters Karana's mind twice while preparing her attack?
3. Tell the unexpected occurrence on the beach.
4. What injury does Karana suffer?
5. Why does she decide to make a home in the cave?

Short Answer Study Guide Questions - *Island of the Blue Dolphins* Page 3

Chapters 13-15 Continued
  6. Describe this cave.
  7. What does Karana find upon returning to the beach?
  8. What is her goal after she has finished making her spears?
  9. After shooting the lead dog with an arrow, what does she do next?
 10. Upon finding the dog she shot lying helplessly, what does she do?

Chapters 16-18
  1. How does Karana redesign the abandoned canoe to meet her needs?
  2. In what ways does Karana find companionship in Rontu?
  3. What do Rontu and Karana discover on their voyage to test the new canoe?
  4. Why does Karana decide to make a special spear during the winter?
  5. How and why does Rontu prove himself?
  6. How does Karana insure that her birds will not fly away?

Chapters 19-21
  1. Explain how a starfish pries open a shell.
  2. How do Karana and Rontu do in the battle with the devilfish?
  3. What does Karana kill at Tall Rock and for what reason?
  4. Why does Karana enter Black Cave?
  5. Describe the figures on the ledge in the cave.
  6. Why do Karana and Rontu spend the night in the cave?
  7. What direction did Karana know the white men's ship would come from?
  8. When she realized an Aleut ship was approaching, what did she do?
  9. How does Karana spend her evenings in the cave while the Aleuts are on the island?
 10. Describe Tutok.
 11. Why does Karana think Tutok wants to know about the cave and her fire?

Chapters 22-25
  1. What does Tutok leave for Karana on the rock?
  2. How do the girls spend their time together?
  3. Why do you think Karana finally shares her secret name with Tutok?
  4. Describe the gift Karana makes for Tutok.
  5. How does Karana feel after Tutok leaves?
  6. Why does Karana rescue an otter?
  7. How does she spend her time that winter?
  8. In what way have Karana's feelings changed about the island animals?
  9. Why did Karana stop counting the moons as they passed?
 10. What painful event occurred late that summer?

Short Answer Study Guide Questions - *Island of the Blue Dolphins* Page 4

Chapters 26-29

1. How does Karana catch Rontu-Aru?
2. Describe the tidal wave.
3. What happened after the crashing waves receded?
4. Who does Karana believe caused the earthquake?
5. While rebuilding a canoe, what does Karana see?
6. Why don't the men from the ship see Karana?
7. How long was it before the ship returned?
8. What does Karana do to prepare to leave the island?
9. Describe the men from the ship.
10. What reaction does Karana have to the sound of the white man's language?
11. What do the men make for Karana before leaving? Why?
12. After reaching the mission, what does Karana learn of the ship that came for her people?

SHORT ANSWER STUDY GUIDE QUESTION ANSWERS
Island of the Blue Dolphins

<u>Author's Note, Chapters 1-3</u>

1. How and when was the island in this story actually discovered by white men?
    In the year 1602, a Spanish explorer sighted the island as he sailed north from Mexico in search of a safe haven for treasure galleons from the Philippines. He named it La Isle de San Nicholas, after the patron saint of sailors, travelers, and merchants.

2. Whose true story is this novel based upon?
    It is based on The Lost Woman of San Nicholas who was found living alone in a crude house with a dog on this island eighteen years after the Indians of Ghalas-at had been rescued.

3. Where is she buried and where was her cormorant skirt sent?
    She is buried on a hill near the Santa Barbara Mission. Her skirt was sent to Rome.

4. How many miles from Los Angeles is San Nicholas?
    It is seventy-five miles southwest of Los Angeles.

5. For what is the island used today?
    It is a secret navel base of the U. S. Navy.

6. What were Ramo and Karana doing when the Aleut ship came?
    The six-year-old Ramo and his twelve-year-old sister were gathering roots.

7. Describe the men rowing the small boat to shore from the ship.
    Six men with broad faces and shining dark hair that fell over their eyes were rowing with long oars. They had bone ornaments thrust through their noses. Behind them stood a tall man with a yellow beard.

8. For what reason had the Russian and his crew come to the island?
    He came with forty men to hunt sea otter. They wish to camp on the island while they hunt.

9. What agreement of payment was reached between the Aleuts and Karana's father, Chief Chowig?
    At first the Russian offered one part for the islanders, to be paid in goods, and two parts for them. He later agreed to equal parts for each.

10. Why do the islanders have a two names, a secret name and a common name?
    The secret name is their real name. If it is used by people it becomes worn out and loses it magic according to Karana.

11. Describe the Island of the Blue Dolphins.
    It is two leagues long and one league wide. If you are standing on one of the hills that rise in the middle of it, the island looks like a dolphin lying on its side with its tail pointing toward the sunrise and its nose pointing to the sunset. Its fins are the reefs and rocky ledges along the shore. The wind blows strongly and constantly causing the hills to be polished smooth and the trees to be small and twisted. The village of Ghalas-at is east of the hills on a small mesa, near Coral Cove and a good spring.

12. What does Chief Chowig order concerning his tribe and the Aleuts?
    He warns everyone against visiting the Aleut camp because he says they are people who do not understand friendship. He remembers an earlier group of Aleuts led by Captain Mitriff who caused great trouble.

13. What good fortune befalls the islanders that spring?
    Karana's older sister, Ulape, spots a school of white bass while searching for shellfish on the eastern part of the island.

14. Give a description of the men who come to ask for fish. Tell the Chief's response.
    They were short-legged men, who only came to Chief Chowig's shoulders, with small eyes like black pebbles and mouths like the edges of a stone knives. The Chief refuses to share the fish with them claiming it is needed by his village people.

15. Describe the sea otters.
    It looks like a seal while swimming, but really has a shorter nose, small webbed feet and fur that is thicker and prettier. It is the most playful animal in the sea, according to Karana.

16. Explain the otter slaughtering process as told by Karana.
    The Aleuts speared the otters from their canoes. At dark they brought their catch in to Coral Cove and skinned and fleshed them on the beach. In the morning the beach would be strewn with carcasses, and the waves red with blood.

17. Why were tribesmen sent to hollow out a log in the cove and sleep beside it at night?
    They were to there to watch the Aleuts, and give alarm if Captain Orlov tried to sail off without paying for the otter skins.

18. Share three observations made by the islanders that indicate the visitors prepare to leave soon.
    The Aleut woman spends a whole afternoon cleaning her skin aprons, the Russian Captain carefully trims his beard so it looks like it did when he arrived, and the spear sharpeners stop their work and spend all their time skinning the otter which were brought in at dusk.

19. What is Karana's father doing at the end of the chapter that leads you to believe he does not trust the agreement?
    He says nothing, but works nightly on a new spear.

Chapters 4-7

1. Why did the tribe hurry to Coral Cove on the sunless day?
   The hunters were packing to leave without having paid for the otter pelts.

2. How many bales of otter pelts had the hunters bundled?
   A total of one hundred twenty bales of otter pelts were bundled; one hundred five already loaded and fifteen still in the cove.

3. What does Chief Chowig agree to do after the other chests are delivered from the ship?
   He claims he will help load the bales of pelts using their canoes.

4. Describe the battle between the hunters and the island warriors.
   Chief Chowig blocked an Aleut hunter's path to a boat; the Chief ended up bloodied on the rocks. He arose and his warriors, with their spears raised, rushed down from the ledge. A cannon was fired from the deck of the ship killing five warriors. The Aleuts drew their knives as the spear-carrying warriors rushed upon them on the shore. Two lines surged back and forth until Captain Orlov, who had rowed to the ship, returned with more Aleuts which forced the warriors backward to the cliffs. The few who were left, continued to fight without retreat. A storm came up, the Aleuts turned and ran to the boat.

5. What do his daughters and the village say weakened Chief Chowig?
   They say he should never have told the Russian his secret name.

6. How many warriors were killed in the battle?
   Twenty-seven of the forty-two men on the island were killed including the Chief.

7. Why did the village wait three days to bury the dead?
   They waited due to the storm.

8. What was done with the dead Aleuts?
   They were burned.

9. Who was named the new chief and why?
   A very old man named Kimki who had been a good man in his youth and a good hunter.

10. How does life change in Ghalas-at?
    Women had to hunt and fish now. The men resented this. Everyone mourned terribly for the dead, it an unpeaceful time.

11. What was Ulape and Karana's job?
    They were to gather abalone.

12. Why does Kimki leave the island in the spring?
    He wanted to go to an island to the east he had been to when he was a boy. He would go there and make a home for the remaining islanders.

13. What is the tribe's plan, under Matasaip's leadership, if the Aleuts return?
    Since they lacked men for defense, the tribe planned to flee to the island of Santa Catalina as soon as the red-sailed ship was sighted. They would all go to the cliff on the south end and let themselves down a rope of bull kelp and leave in their canoes, which had food and water stored in them.

14. Nanko brings what news?
    The sighted ship is not the dreaded Aleuts, but a ship of white men that Kimki has sent for them.

15. How does Ulape, preparing for the voyage, indicate she is unmarried?
    She draws a thin mark of blue clay across her nose and cheekbones.

16. Why had Ramo missed the boat?
    He had forgotten his fishing spear.

17. What does Karana do when she realizes the ship is not returning for her brother?
    She flings herself into the sea and swims for shore, ruining her beautiful skirt of yucca fibers which she had donned for the trip.

Chapters 8, 9

1. Where does Ramo go alone against Karana's instructions?
   He went to the south part of the island, near the cliff, where the canoes are hidden.

2. What happens to him?
   The wild dogs attacked and killed him.

3. After this has happened to Ramo, what does Karana vow?
   She vows to kill the wild dogs.

4. How does Karana end the haunting village's sights and sounds?
    She burns the village down, hut by hut.

5. Why does she search for weapons that may have been left behind?
    She needs them for protection for the laws of Ghalas-at forbade the making of weapons by women.

6. What is she looking for in the chest left by the Aleuts? What does she find?
    She went looking for iron spearheads. She finds in it beads, bracelets, and earrings of many colors.

7. Karana fears bad things may happen to her. Why ?
    She fears she will punished if she makes or uses weapons because she is a female.

8. What makes her decide to go against the tribe's law?
    The wild dogs, who killed Ramo keep returning.

9. Why is it difficult for her to make the weapons?
    Even though she had watched her father make them , she only watched with the eye of someone who would never do it.

10. How does she make her rock bed on the headland more comfortable?
    She carried dry seaweed up from the beach.

Chapters 10-12
1. Why is Karana losing hope of a ship returning?
    Many seasons had passed and the time of good weather when she thought they would have come had passed.

2. What decision has Karana made during the storm?
    She would take one of the canoes and go to the country that lay toward the east.

3. How does she feel about her decision?
    Whatever might befall her on the endless water did not trouble her as much as staying on the island alone.

4. What lessens her fears while on the sea at night?
    Familiar stars begin to appear in the night sky.

5. What problem develops and how does she solve it?
    She finds her canoe is leaking so she tore fiber from her skirt to stuff into the hole.

6. Why does she decide to turn back for the island?
    The leaks grow worse and she has at least two more days to go.

7. How do the dolphins influence Karana?
    She feels as if she had friends with her so she was not so lonely and afraid. They are a good omen.

8. In what way do Karana's feelings change when she returns to the island?
    She was happy to be home. Everything she saw filled her with happiness.

9. What does she decide she must do first? What requirements are there?
    She must build a house. It needs to be sheltered from the wind, close to Coral Cove, and close to a good spring.

10. Out of what does Karana build a fence?
    She uses whale ribs bound by strands of bull kelp.

11. Describe the house she builds.
    She chooses a rock for the back end and lines up four poles on each side, bound together with sinew and covered with broad-leafed female kelp. She has eight poles on top, bound and covered the same way.

12. How is Karana able to work at night with no sunlight?
    She catches basketfuls of sai-sai, dries them and burns them at night.

13. What does Karana require for her spear?
    She needs the tooth of a bull sea elephant for the point.

Chapters 13-15

1. Describe the cow, bull, and baby sea elephants.
    The cow has a smooth body and a face that looks like that of a mouse. The bull's face has a large hump on it which hangs down over his mouth. His skin is rough and cracked; an ugly animal. The babies are a large as a man, waddling along on flippers.

2. What warning of her father's enters Karana's mind twice while preparing her attack?
    She fears her bow will break in a time of danger because she is a woman.

3. Tell the unexpected occurrence on the beach.
    There is a battle between a young bull and an old bull.

4. What injury does Karana suffer?
    In haste to get out the way of the old bull, she tripped over a stone and fell to her knees.

5. Why does she decide to make a home in the cave?
    It is a safe place near a spring.

6. Describe this cave.
    There were carved figures in the stone on either side of the walls. Near the opening there were two cut basins.

7. What does Karana find upon returning to the beach?
    She finds the bones of the old bull, taking the teeth.

8. What is her goal after she has finished making her spears?
    She will go to the cave of the wild dogs to kill them.

9. After shooting the lead dog with an arrow, what does she do next?
    She kills two more of the dogs. She then ventures into their cave and finds a half-eaten fox carcass near a mother dog and her litter of four pups.

10. Upon finding the dog she shot lying helplessly, what does she do?
    She picks him up, removes the arrow point, and cleanses his wound. She leaves him water and eventually feeds him. After four days, they become friends. She names him Rontu.

Chapters 16-18

1. How does Karana redesign the abandoned canoe to meet her needs?
    She loosened all the planks, cut them to half their length, and bound them back together.

2. In what ways does Karana find companionship in Rontu?
    He stayed with her at all times and she often spoke to him.

3. What do Rontu and Karana discover on their voyage to test the new canoe?
    A hiding place for her canoe in a sea cave near the headland and a devilfish.

4. Why does Karana decide to make a special spear during the winter?
    A special kind of spear is needed to catch the devilfish.

5. Why doesn't Karana shoot the wild dogs who are Rontu's rivals?
    She knew the battle was between Rontu and these dogs; if she interfered they would still fight, just at another time and place, maybe one less favorable to Rontu.

6. How does Karana insure that her birds will not fly away?
    She clips their wings.

Chapters 19-21

1. Explain how a starfish pries open an abalone shell.
    After it places itself over the shell, it holds it with its suckers and begins to lift itself. It continues to hold on, pulling against the abalone, until little by little the shell comes loose from the body.

2. How do Karana and Rontu do in the battle with the devilfish?
    It is a fierce and tiresome battle. Both Rontu and Karana are wrapped with the devilfish's leech-like arms at some point. She ultimately kills it, although she is too weak to drag it home. She salvages only her weapon.

3. What does Karana kill at Tall Rock and for what reason?
    She kills ten cormorants from which she will make a skirt.

4. Why does Karana enter Black Cave?
    She sees a hawk fly out of it and is curious.

5. Describe the figures on the ledge in the cave.
    There were two dozen figures as tall as Karana with long legs and arms and short bodies made of reeds and clothed in gull feathers. Each one had eyes fashioned from abalone shells.

6. Why do Karana and Rontu spend the night in the cave?
    The tide had come in and there was not enough space for them to exit out of the opening.

7. What direction did Karana know the white men's ship would come from?
    It would come from the east.

8. When she realized an Aleut ship was approaching, what did she do?
    She packed up her belongings and moved to the cave near the ravine.

9. How does Karana spend her evenings in the cave while the Aleuts are on the island?
    She works on her cormorant skirt.

10. Describe Tutok.
    She is less tall than Karana with a broad face and small black eyes. Her teeth are worn down from chewing seal sinew, but are very white.

11. Why does Karana think Tutok wants to know about the cave and her fire?
    She fears she will bring the Aleuts back to capture her and harm her.

Chapters 22-25
1. What does Tutok leave for Karana on the rock?
    She leaves a beautiful, black stone necklace.

2. How do the girls spend their time together?
    They communicate; pointing things out to each other using their language, laugh, and exchange gifts.

3. Why do you think Karana finally shares her secret name with Tutok?
    She has come to like and trust Tutok.

4. Describe the gift Karana makes for Tutok.
    It is a circlet made of abalone and olivella shells threaded together with sinew.

5. How does Karana feel after Tutok leaves?
    She misses her and even though she hears the sounds of the island, it seems very quiet with Tutok gone.

6. Why does Karana rescue an otter?
    A strand of kelp is wrapped around its body in the kelp bed, and it has a deep gash across its back.

7. How does she spend her time that winter?
    She searches the beach for matching stones to make earrings to go with the black stone necklace Tutok gave her. On sunny days she would wear the earrings, necklace, and her cormorant skirt and walk along the cliff with Rontu wishing Tutok were there to see her and to talk with her.

8. In what way have Karana's feelings changed about the island animals?
    She would not kill another living thing for they had become her friends or could become her friends. She comes to believe animals and birds are like people too, though they do not talk the same or do the same things.

9. Why did Karana stop counting the moons as they passed?
    The passing of the moons had come to mean little; she began to only make marks to count the four seasons of the year.

10. What painful event occurred late that summer?
    Rontu, her dog, died.

Chapters 26-29

1. How does Karana catch Rontu-Aru?
    She mixes up a potion that will cause the dogs to sleep and puts it in the spring. After he drinks from the spring and is asleep, she drags him to her house where she ties him with a thong and leaves him with food and water. In a short time, they become friends.

2. Describe the tidal wave.
    For days the weather had become very hot and windless. Suddenly, there was a loud rumbling and the tide was exceptionally low. The air became tight, with a sucking sound, and then a great white crest from the sea advanced toward the island. It crashed and then as it receded, another came and they collided.

3. What happened after the crashing waves receded?
    It became still and hot again, until the earthquake.

4. Who does Karana believe caused the earthquake?
    She thinks it was caused by gods, the ones who make the earth shake.

5. While rebuilding a canoe, what does Karana see?
    She sees a ship heading toward the island.

6. Why don't the men from the ship see Karana?
    Their canoe had gone back to the ship. The wind was screaming, mist was blowing in, and the waves were crashing in to the shore while Karana tried to get their attention.

7. How long was it before the ship returned?
    Two more springs had gone. (2 years)

8. What does Karana do to prepare to leave the island?
    First she goes to the spring to bath. Then she puts on her otter cape, cormorant skirt, and black stone necklace and earrings. With blue clay she makes the mark of her tribe across her nose and also makes the sign that she is unmarried. She cooks a meal for herself and Rontu-Aru and fills her three baskets. She gets her cage with two young birds, as well.

9. Describe the men from the ship.
    There were two tall men and one short one clothed in a long gray robe. The man in the robe had a string of beads around his neck that had an ornament of polished wood at the end of it.

10. What reaction does Karana have to the sound of the white man's language?
    She thinks they sound very strange and wants to laugh at them at first. Then she realizes the sound of a human voice is as sweet as no sound in the world.

11. What do the men make for Karana before leaving?
    They make her a blue dress from their trousers that reaches from her throat to her feet.

12. After reaching the mission, what news does Karana learn of the ship that came for her people?
    The ship had sunk in a great storm soon after it reached the mission.

MULTIPLE CHOICE STUDY GUIDE/QUIZ QUESTIONS - *Island of the Blue Dolphins*

Author's Note, Chapters 1-3

1. The island in this story was discovered in 1602 by
    a. Father Gonzales.
    b. Sebastian Vizcaino.
    c. Christopher Columbus.
    d. Saint Nicholas.

2. This novel is based on the true story of
    a. The Lost Woman of San Nicholas.
    b. La Brea Woman.
    c. Ghalas-at Girl.
    d. Robin Crusett.

3. The female this story is about is buried
    a. in Los Angeles.
    b. on the island of San Nicholas.
    c. near Santa Barbara Mission.
    d. on Santa Catalina.

4. San Nicholas is how far from Los Angeles?
    a. It is seven hundred miles.
    b. It is seventy-five miles.
    c. It is seventeen leagues.
    d. It is seventy- five kilometers.

5. Located on the island today is a
    a. Marine Biology Site.
    b. Sea Animal Conservation Colony.
    c. U. S. Naval Base.
    d. Environmental Study Region.

6. When the Aleut ship arrived Karana and Ramo were
    a. searching for shellfish.
    b. scaring away the gulls.
    c. collecting abalone shells.
    d. gathering roots.

7. Other than the six dark -haired men with broad faces and bone ornaments through their noses, who else was in the boat?
    a. There was an Aleut woman.
    b. There was a priest.
    c. There was a tall man with a yellow beard.
    d. There was a golden-haired dog.

Study Guide/Quiz Questions *Island of the Blue Dolphins* Multiple Choice Format Page 2

8. The Russian and his crew came to the island to
    a. hunt sea otter.
    b. hunt dolphins.
    c. hunt cormorants.
    d. hunt sea elephants.

9. The payment agreement decided upon between Chief Chowig and the Aleuts was
    a. one part for the natives, two parts for the Aleuts.
    b. nothing for the natives.
    c. four beads per pelt for the natives.
    d. equal parts for each party.

10. The islanders have
    a. nicknames.
    b. holiday names.
    c. gods' names.
    d. none of the above

11. The Island of the Blue Dolphins mostly resembles
    a. a mesa.
    b. a dolphin.
    c. a sea elephant.
    d. a kelp bed.

12. Chief Chowig warns his tribe
    a. to watch the visitors day and night.
    b. count the otter pelts.
    c. not to visit the Aleut camp.
    d. to gather as much food as possible before bad weather arrives.

13. Good fortune befalls the islanders that spring because Ulape
    a. discovers a great shellfish spot.
    b. befriends the Aleut woman.
    c. finds the lost cave.
    d. spots a school of white bass.

14. When the black-eyed, short-legged men come to ask for fish, the Chief
    a. refuses.
    b. tells them his village needs them.
    c. sends a response to the Russian.
    d. all of the above

Study Guide/Quiz Questions *Island of the Blue Dolphins* Multiple Choice Format Page 3

15. Sea otters resemble seals except for their
    a. shorter noses and thicker fur.
    b. fins.
    c. longer tails.
    d. shinier skin.

16. Otter slaughtering involves
    a. catching them with nets.
    b. spearing them from canoes.
    c. boiling the pelts.
    d. luring them to the shore.

17. Tribesmen were sent to hollow out a log in the cove and sleep beside it at night because
    a. they were the most skilled.
    b. seldom do trees wash ashore.
    c. they feared Orlov's men would take the tree for themselves.
    d. they were to watch in case Orlov tried to sneak away at night.

18. Select the one behavior not representative of the Aleuts readying to leave.
    a. The Aleut woman spends a whole afternoon cleaning her skin apron.
    b. The hunters brought their catch into Coral Cove.
    c. The Russian Captain carefully trims his beard so it looks like it did when he arrived.
    d. The spear sharpeners stop their work and spend all their time skinning the otter.

19. At the end of the chapter, Karana's father
    a. hopes to meet the single Aleut woman.
    b. helps the Aleuts load the pelts.
    c. works nightly on a new spear.
    d. waits confidently for the Russian's payment.

Study Guide/Quiz Questions *Island of the Blue Dolphins* Multiple Choice Format Page 4

<u>Chapters 4-7</u>
1. The tribe hurried to Coral Cove on the sunless day because
   a. a storm was brewing.
   b. the hunters were unloading the chests full of trinkets.
   c. the Chief ordered the tribe to help clean the beach.
   d. the hunters were packing to leave without having paid for the otter pelts.

2. How many total bales of otter pelts had the hunters bundled?
   a. They had one hundred twenty.
   b. They had fifty.
   c. They had one hundred fifty.
   d. They had one hundred five.

3. After the other chests are delivered from the ship, Chief Chowig agrees to
   a. send food with the crew.
   b. help load the bales of pelts using their canoes.
   c. share the profit.
   d. send tribesmen with them to help guide the ship.

4. Which event *did not* occur in the battle between the hunters and the island warriors?
   a. Chief Chowig blocked a hunter's path.
   b. Aleut ship fired a cannon from its deck.
   c. Orlov returned with more hunters.
   d. none of the above

5. The village says Chief Chowig was weakened by
   a. the hard winter.
   b. mourning his wife's recent death.
   c. telling the Russian his secret name.
   d. the loss of all of the otters.

6. How many warriors were killed in the battle?
   a. Twenty-seven were killed.
   b. Forty-two were killed.
   c. Fifteen were killed.
   d. Thirty-five were killed.

7. How many days did the storm last causing the tribe to forestall burying their dead?
   a. It lasted four days.
   b. It lasted two days.
   c. It lasted three days.
   d. none of the above

Study Guide/Quiz Questions *Island of the Blue Dolphins* Multiple Choice Format Page 5

8. The dead Aleuts on the beach were
    a. left for the vultures.
    b. thrown in the sea.
    c. buried.
    d. burned.

9. The new chief chosen by the council to replace Chowig was
    a. Matasaip.
    b. Kimki.
    c. Ramo.
    d. Nanko.

10. The major change in Ghalas-at is
    a. women must do men's jobs.
    b. children must now hunt.
    c. men must do women's jobs.
    d. all must pray at dawn to be spared from another attack.

11. Ulape and Karana's job is to
    a. watch for any approaching ships.
    b. locate the wild dogs' lair.
    c. scare the gulls away from the food.
    d. collect abalone shells.

12. Kimki leaves the island in the spring to
    a. go off to die where he was born.
    b. discover a new island.
    c. find a new source of food.
    d. make a new home for the islanders.

13. If the Aleuts return
    a. the village plans to flee.
    b. the men will defend the island.
    c. the tribe will hide.
    d. none of the above

14. Nanko brings news of
    a. a ship of white men sent by Kimki.
    b. an approaching Aleut ship.
    c. Kimki's return.
    d. a tidal wave.

Study Guide/Quiz Questions *Island of the Blue Dolphins* Multiple Choice Format Page 6

15. Ulape draws a thin mark of blue clay across her nose and cheekbones to indicate
    a. she is married.
    b. she is the daughter of the chief.
    c. she is unmarried.
    d. she is in mourning.

16. Ramo missed the boat because he went back for his fishing spear.
    a. false
    b. true

17. When Karana realizes the ship is not returning for her brother she
    a. begs Ulape to come back with her.
    b. hops in a canoe and rows back to the island.
    c. jumps into the sea, swimming for shore.
    d. forces the ship captain to return

Study Guide/Quiz Questions *Island of the Blue Dolphins* Multiple Choice Format Page 7

<u>Chapters 8, 9</u>
1. Against Karana's orders, Ramo goes to
    a. where the canoes are hidden on the south end of the island.
    b. where their father is buried.
    c. Coral Cove to watch for the returning ship.
    d. none of the above

2. When Karana finds Ramo he
    a. has news of the returning ship.
    b. wants to share his abalones with her.
    c. has found the canoe and is trying to drag it back to her.
    d. has been killed by the wild dogs.

3. Karana now vows to
    a. find the Aleut chest.
    b. leave the island.
    c. kill the wild dogs.
    d. all of the above

4. To end the haunting reminder of the village people, Karana
    a. moves there to be among her ancestors.
    b. burns it down.
    c. goes to the other end of the island to live.
    d. none of the above

5. She searches for weapons that may have been left behind because
    a. she needs them for protection.
    b. the laws of Ghalas-at forbid women from making weapons.
    c. she doesn't have any.
    d. all of the above

6. Karana finds in the chest left by the Aleuts
    a. iron spearheads.
    b. beads and bracelets.
    c. earrings.
    d. both b and c

7. Karana fears bad things may happen to her because
    a. she is all alone.
    b. she has seen the god of death.
    c. she is a women who makes and uses weapons.
    d. the ship has not returned.

Study Guide/Quiz Questions *Island of the Blue Dolphins* Multiple Choice Format Page 8

8. What makes her decide to go against the tribe's law?
    a. She sees no sign of the returning ship.
    b. The wild dogs, who killed Ramo keep returning.
    c. She needs something to do with her time.
    d. She decides the laws of her tribe are outdated

9. Why is it difficult for her to make the weapons?
    a. She has never made them before.
    b. Women don't do such things.
    c. She has not watched her father very carefully when he made them.
    d. All of the above

10. To make her rock bed softer, Karana uses cormorant feathers.
    a. true
    b. false

Study Guide/Quiz Questions- *Island of the Blue Dolphins* Multiple Choice Format Page 9

Chapters 10-12

1. Karana is losing hope of the ship returning because
    a. the god of the underground appeared to her.
    b. many seasons have passed.
    c. the time of good weather has passed.
    d. both b and c

2. During the storm, Karana has decided to
    a. take one of the canoes and go to the country that lay toward the east.
    b. move to the cave.
    c. try to develop smoke signals using seaweed from the beach.
    d. make weapons for her protection.

3. Her feeling about her decision is
    a. fearlessness.
    b. cautiousness.
    c. loneliness.
    d. all of the above

4. Her fears are lessened while on the sea at night by
    a. the dolphins.
    b. familiar stars.
    c. the rhythm of the waves.
    d. the sight of land.

5. How does she solve her developing problem?
    a. She places her baskets over the leak.
    b. She tears fiber from her skirt and stuffs it into the leak.
    c. She sits in a different position so the leak doesn't ever hit the water.
    d. She uses a different paddle and places the paddle over the leak.

6. She decides to turn back for the island because
    a. she gives up hope.
    b. she is certain she can find her way back there.
    c. the leaks grow worse and she has a far distance yet to go.
    d. the dolphins signal her to return.

7. How do the dolphins influence Karana?
    a. They are a good omen.
    b. She feels less lonely.
    c. She feels less afraid.
    d. All of the above

Study Guide/Quiz Questions- *Island of the Blue Dolphins* Multiple Choice Format Page 10

8. In what way do Karana's feelings change when she returns to the island?
    a. She was happy to be home.
    b. Everything she saw filled her with happiness.
    c. She hugs the sand.
    d. All of the above.

9. Which is *not* one of the requirements for Karana's house?
    a. It needs to be on the headland.
    b. It needs to be close to a good spring.
    c. It needs to be close to Coral Cove.
    d. It needs to be sheltered from the wind.

10. Karana builds a fence out of
    a. broken canoes.
    b. remnants of the huts in the village.
    c. whale ribs.
    d. none of the above

11. Choose the one thing *not true* of the house Karana builds.
    a. The back end is a large rock.
    b. The roof is made of poles covered with seaweed.
    c. The sides are made of large rocks.
    d. None of the above

12. Karana is able to work at night with no sunlight because she
    a. burns her oil lamp.
    b. burns little dried fish.
    c. uses the embers from the day fire.
    d. works when there is a full moon.

13. For her spear, Karana requires a
    a. whale rib.
    b. pelican tooth.
    c. bull sea elephant tooth.
    d. very sharp abalone shell.

Study Guide/Quiz Questions *Island of the Blue Dolphins* Multiple Choice Format Page 11

Chapters 13-15

1. The cow, bull, and baby sea elephants are identical.
    a. true
    b. false

2. Her father's warning that her bow will break in a time of danger
    a. enters her mind twice during her attack.
    b. causes her not to attack.
    c. never enters her mind.
    d. causes her to aim incorrectly.

3. There is an unexpected battle between a young bull and an old bull on the beach.
    a. true
    b. false

4. What injury does Karana suffer?
    a. She hurt her back falling on the slippery rocks.
    b. She dislocated her shoulder pulling back her bow.
    c. She fell to the ground hurting her leg.
    d. None of the above

5. She decides to make a second home in the cave because
    a. it will be safe.
    b. it is near a spring.
    c. it is warmer.
    d. both a and b

6. The most interesting feature of the cave is
    a. the stone basins.
    b. the stalactites.
    c. the ancient wall carvings.
    d. the stalagmites.

7. Upon returning to the beach, Karana finds
    a. one bull sea elephant tooth.
    b. the bones of the sea elephant.
    c. many bull sea elephant teeth.
    d. all of the above

8. What will she do now that she has what she wants?
    a. She will go to the cave of the wild dogs to kill them
    b. She will wait for the ship to return.
    c. She will kill many otters for a new cape.
    d. She will spear the devilfish.

Study Guide/Quiz Questions- *Island of the Blue Dolphins* Multiple Choice Format Page 12

9. After shooting the lead dog with an arrow, she
    a. kills two more of the dogs.
    b. ventures into their cave
    c. finds a mother dog and its litter
    d. all of the above

10. Which of the following *doesn't* Karana do upon finding the lead dog she shot?
    a. She carries him to her place.
    b. She tries to heal him with a coral bush.
    c. She shoots him again with her sharpest arrow.
    d. She gives him food and water.

Study Guide/Quiz Questions- *Island of the Blue Dolphins* Multiple Choice Format Page 13

Chapters 16-18
1. Karana redesigns the canoe because it
    a. has rotted out.
    b. is too large for her to handle.
    c. isn't large enough for Rontu and her.
    d. needs new pitch on the bottom.

2. Karana finds friendship through Rontu by
    a. affection.
    b. conversation.
    c. companionship.
    d. all of the above

3. While testing the newly designed canoe, Rontu and Karana find a
    a. whale.
    b. devilfish.
    c. cormorant.
    d. pelican.

4. Karana decides to make a special spear to
    a. kill the whale.
    b. kill the devilfish.
    c. kill the wild dogs.
    d. kill the otters.

5. Karana doesn't kill Rontu's rivals because she doesn't believe in killing anymore.
    a. true
    b. false

6. Karana clips the birds wings to keep them from flying away.
    a. true
    b. false

Study Guide/Quiz Questions- *Island of the Blue Dolphins* Multiple Choice Format Page 14

Chapters 19-21

1. It is a quick and easy process for a starfish to pry open an abalone shell.
    a. true
    b. false

2. Karana and Rontu have a difficult time spearing the devilfish but proudly carry it home to eat its delicious, tender meat.
    a. true
    b. false

3. What does Karana kill at Tall Rock?
    a. otters
    b. cormorants
    c. yucca
    d. seals

4. Karana enters Black Cave because
    a. she sees a hawk fly out of it and is curious.
    b. she sees a sparkling shimmer reflecting on the water.
    c. she has always wanted to go into it.
    d. Rontu barks and leans towards it.

5. The two dozen figures on the ledge in the cave are
    a. clothed in gull feathers.
    b. abalone shell- eyed.
    c. made of reeds.
    d. all of the above

6. Karana and Rontu spend the night in the cave because
    a. they like the adventure.
    b. Rontu will not get out of the canoe.
    c. the tide has come in and there is not enough space for them to exit out of the opening.
    d. they find lots of abalones and need the following daylight to load them into the canoe.

7. Karana knew the white men's ship would come from the
    a. east
    b. west
    c. north
    d. south

Study Guide/Quiz Questions- *Island of the Blue Dolphins* Multiple Choice Format Page 15

8. When Karana realizes an Aleut ship is approaching she
    a. runs to the south end of the island for one of the canoes.
    b. goes to the cliff to see if they are the same ones who killed her father.
    c. packs up her belongings and moves to the cave near the ravine.
    d. hides behind rock in the harbor.

9. While the Aleuts are on the island, Karana spends her evenings in the cave
    a. working on her cormorant skirt.
    b. praying to the gods of the stars.
    c. drying sai-sai to burn later when they leave.
    d. learning to play a flute made from a pelican bone.

10. Tutok is
    a. less tall than Karana.
    b. taller than Karana.
    c. brown-eyed.
    d. younger than Karana.

11. Karana thinks Tutok wants to know about the cave and her fire so she can bring the other Aleuts to find her and capture her.
    a. true
    b. false

Study Guide/Quiz Questions-*Island of the Blue Dolphins* Multiple Choice Format Page 16

Chapters 22-25

1. What does Tutok leave for Karana on the rock?
    a. She leaves an abalone shell necklace.
    b. She leaves a set of hair combs made from gull feathers.
    c. She leaves a black stone necklace.
    d. all of the above

2. The girls spend their time together
    a. laughing.
    b. crying.
    c. communicating in their native languages.
    d. both a and c

3. Karana shares her secret name with Tutok the first time they exchange names.
    a. true
    b. false

4. The gift Karana makes for Tutok
    a. is very similar to the gift Tutok gave Karana.
    b. is the wrong size for Tutok's small head.
    c. is a circlet made of abalone and olivella shells threaded together with sinew.
    d. none of the above

5. After Tutok leaves, Karana
    a. misses her company and voice.
    b. pretends she is talking with her, making things up to talk about.
    c. thinks the island sounds are very quiet.
    d. all of the above

6. Karana rescues an otter because
    a. it is crying out to her.
    b. Rontu has scared it badly.
    c. it is injured and scared.
    d. it has been left to die by the Aleuts.

7. Karana spends her time that winter
    a. searching for matching black stones for earrings.
    b. walking along the sandspit.
    c. walking with Rontu along the cliff.
    d. both a and c

Study Guide/Quiz Questions-*Island of the Blue Dolphins* Multiple Choice Format Page 17

8. Karana's feelings changed about the island animals.
    a. true
    b. false

9. Karana stops counting the moons as they passed because
    a. it came to mean very little to her.
    b. she had forgotten the symbol for it.
    c. they came and went so swiftly.
    d. she wanted to forget how long she had been alone.

10. What painful event occurred late that summer?
    a. Her birds flew away.
    b. Rontu died.
    c. The otters left the island.
    d. There was another sea elephant mating battle.

Study Guide/Quiz Questions-*Island of the Blue Dolphins* Multiple Choice Format Page 18

Chapters 26-29

1. Karana catches Rontu-Aru by
     a. chasing him around the island.
     b. drugging him and then carrying him back to her place.
     c. luring him into a snare and waiting until he was very hungry and thirsty.
     d. none of the above

2. Select the one inaccurate description of the tidal wave's warning.
     a. extremely low tide
     b. heavy air
     c. dark sky
     d. blinding light

3. After the crashing waves receded
     a. there was an earthquake.
     b. there was a cool wind.
     c. there was another tidal wave.
     d. there was a new, bluer sky above.

4. Who does Karana believe caused the earthquake?
     a. She thinks it was caused by the sea caves expanding from the heat.
     b. She thinks the trees that went underground are trying to reroot.
     c. She thinks it was caused by gods who make the earth shake.
     d. She thinks her weapon-making has caused the earthquake.

5. While rebuilding a canoe, Karana sees
     a. an Aleut ship.
     b. a whale spouting.
     c. another ship.
     d. the white-sailed ship that took her people.

6. The men do not see or hear Karana because
     a. their canoe has returned to the ship.
     b. the waves are crashing against the shore.
     c. the wind is screaming.
     d. all of the above

7. How long was it before the ship returned?
     a. two seasons
     b. two years
     c. two springs
     d. two moons

Study Guide/Quiz Questions-*Island of the Blue Dolphins* Multiple Choice Format Page 19

8. What does Karana *not* do to prepare to leave the island?
    a. She marks her face with the sign of her tribe.
    b. She puts on her necklace, earrings, cape, and skirt.
    c. She fills her canoe with her things.
    d. She gathers her caged birds.

9. Select the one that describes one of the men from the ship.
    a. dark-skinned
    b. medium height
    c. dressed in a long gray robe
    d. none of the above

10. Karana is at first amused by the white man's speech, but then is comforted by its sound, the sound of a human voice.
    a. true
    b. false

11. The men make for Karana a
    a. cape.
    b. pair of shoes.
    c. dress.
    d. cross.

12. Father Gonzales tells Karana that the ship her people came over on
    a. was preserved in a museum in San Diego.
    b. sunk in a tidal wave right after it left her island.
    c. was sent to Africa for slave trading.
    d. sunk in a great storm shortly after it made it to the mission.

ANSWER KEY: MULTIPLE CHOICE STUDY GUIDE QUESTIONS
Island of the Blue Dolphins

<u>Author's Note Ch.1-3</u>
1. B   15. A
2. A   16. A
3. C   17. D
4. B   18. B
5. C   19. C
6. D
7. C
8. A
9. D
10. D
11. B
12. C
13. D
14. D

<u>Ch-4-7</u>
1. D   15. C
2. A   16. B
3. B   17. C
4. D
5. C
6. A
7. C
8. D
9. B
10. A
11. D
12. D
13. A
14. A

<u>Ch. 8, 9</u>
1. A
2. D
3. C
4. B
5. D
6. D
7. C
8. B
9. D
10. B

<u>Ch. 10-12</u>
1. D
2. A
3. D
4. B
5. B
6. C
7. D
8. D
9. A
10. C
11. C
12. B
13. C

<u>Ch. 13-15</u>
1. B
2. A
3. A
4. C
5. D
6. C
7. D
8. A
9. D
10. C

<u>Ch. 16-18</u>
1. B
2. D
3. B
4. B
5. B
6. A

<u>Ch. 19-21</u>
1. B   11. A
2. B
3. B
4. A
5. C
6. C
7. A
8. C
9. A
10. A
11. A

<u>Ch. 22-25</u>
1. C
2. D
3. B
4. C
5. D
6. C
7. D
8. A
9. A
10. B

<u>Ch. 26-29</u>
1. B
2. C
3. A
4. C
5. C
6. D
7. C
8. C
9. C
10. A
11. C
12. D

PREREADING VOCABULARY WORKSHEETS

Vocabulary - *Island of the Blue Dolphins* Author's Note and Chapters 1-3

Part I: Using Prior Knowledge and Contextual Clues
Below are the sentences in which the vocabulary words appear in the text. Read the sentence. Use any clues you can find in the sentence combined with your prior knowledge, and write what you think the underlined words mean on the lines provided.

1. In that year the Spanish explorer Sebastian Vizcaino set out from Mexico in search of a port where treasure *galleons* from the Philippines could find shelter in case of distress.

2. We know that the girl did jump into the sea, despite efforts to *restrain* her.

3. Recent carbon-14 tests of *excavations* on the island show that Indians came here from the north long before the Christian era.

4. I am deeply indebted to Fletcher Carr, formerly *curator* of the San Diego Museum of Man.

5. "Not on the sea," I said. "Dolphins sit there, and gulls, and *cormorants*, and otter, and whales too, but not clouds.

6. By the time I had filled the basket, the Aleut ship had sailed around the wide *kelp* bed that encloses our island and between the two rocks that guard Coral Cove.

7. Our women were gathering at the edge of the *mesa*.

8. I made my way through the heavy brush and, moving swiftly, down the *ravine* until I came to the sea cliffs.

9. The rest were concealed among the rocks at the foot of the trail, ready to attack the *intruders* should they prove unfriendly.

10. "I come in peace and wish to *parley*," he said to the men on the shore.

11. "From here to the coast of Santa Barbara- twenty *leagues* away?"

Blue Dolphins Vocabulary Note Through Chapter 3 Continued

Part II: Determining the Meaning   Match the vocabulary words to their dictionary definitions.

____ 1. galleons   A. steep-sided high flat land
____ 2. restrain   B. meet; hold a discussion
____ 3. excavations   C. person in charge of a museum
____ 4. curator   D. control; hold back
____ 5. cormorants   E. trespassers
____ 6. kelp   F. large sailing vessels
____ 7. mesa   G. large, web-footed sea birds
____ 8. ravine   H. coarse, brown seaweed
____ 9. intruders   I. long, deep hollow in ground made by a stream
____10. parley   J. digs
____11. leagues   K. three miles unit of measure

Vocabulary - *Island of the Blue Dolphins* Chapters 4-7

Part I: Using Prior Knowledge and Contextual Clues

Below are the sentences in which the vocabulary words appear in the text. Read the sentence. Use any clues you can find in the sentence combined with your prior knowledge, and write what you think the underlined words mean on the lines provided.

1., 2. "There will be *shirkers* who will be punished, for without the help of all, all must *perish*."

3. Kimki portioned work for each one in the tribe, giving Ulape and me the task of gathering *abalones.*

4. There was much trouble over this until Kimki *decreed* that the work would again be divided- henceforth the men would hunt and the women harvest.

5. "There are other things more important to *ponder*," said Matasaip who had taken Kimki's place.

6. I took my skirt of *yucca* fiber, however, for I had spent many days making it and it was very pretty and also my otter cape.

7. Ulape had two boxes of earrings, for she was *vainer* than I, and when she put them into her baskets, she drew a thin mark with blue clay across her nose and cheekbones.

8. I kept thinking over and over as I swam how I would punish Ramo when I reached the shore, yet when I felt the sand under my feet and saw him standing at the edge of the waves, holding his fishing spear and looking so *forlorn*, I forgot all those things I planned to do.

Part II: Determining the Meaning   Match the vocabulary words to their dictionary definitions.

___ 12. shirkers
___ 13. perish
___ 14. abalones
___ 15. decreed
___ 16. ponder
___ 17. yucca
___ 18. vainer
___ 19. forlorn

A. ordered
B. loafers
C. miserable
D. think about
E. die
F. plant with stiff pointy leaves
G. edible shellfish whose shell is lined with mother-of-pearl
H. more self-important

Vocabulary - *Island of the Blue Dolphins* Chapters 8, 9

Part I: Using Prior Knowledge and Contextual Clues
Below are the sentences in which the vocabulary words appear in the text. Read the sentence. Use any clues you can find in the sentence combined with your prior knowledge, and write what you think the underlined words mean on the lines provided.

1. But when the sun rose and I went out of the hut, the pack trotted off toward its *lair* which was at the north side of the island, in a large cave.

2. As is the custom, therefore, I will have to whip you with a switch of *nettles* and then tie you to a red-ant hill"

3. Two trails led there, one on each side of a long sand *dune*.

4. The laws of Ghalas-at *forbade* the making of weapons by women of the tribe, so I went out to search for any that might have been left behind.

5. I held each of the *trinkets* to the sun, turning them so that they caught the light.

6. That night they came back to the *headland.*

7. This I bound to a long shaft, with the green *sinews* of a seal I killed with a rock.

8. In the morning the gulls flew out from their nests in the *crevices* of the cliff.

Part II: Determining the Meaning.   Match the vocabulary words to their dictionary definitions.

___ 20. lair   A. rounded hill of sand formed by the wind
___ 21. nettles   B. a high point of land or rock extending into a large body of water
___ 22. dune   C. narrow openings
___ 23. forbade   D. outlawed
___ 24. trinkets   E. baubles; jewels
___ 25. headland   F. plants armed with stinging hairs
___ 26. sinews   G. den of wild animals
___ 27. crevices   H. tendons

Vocabulary - *Island of the Blue Dolphins* Chapters 10-12

Part I: Using Prior Knowledge and Contextual Clues
Below are the sentences in which the vocabulary words appear in the text. Read the sentence. Use any clues you can find in the sentence combined with your prior knowledge, and write what you think the underlined words mean on the lines provided.

1. Kneeling in the middle of the canoe, I paddled hard and did not pause until I had gone through the tides that run fast around the *sandspit*.

2. The places between the planks were filled with black *pitch* which we gather along the shore.

3. Dolphins are animals of good *omen*.

4. It made me happy to see them swimming around the canoe, and though my hands had begun to bleed from the *chafing* of the paddle, just watching them made me forget the pain.

5. The spring was better than the one near the headland, being less *brackish* and having a steadier flow of water.

6. At dawn when the *clamor* started again I left and went back to the headland.

7. I would have used seal sinew to bind the ribs together, for this is stronger than kelp, but wild animals like it and soon would have *gnawed* the fence down.

8. By heating small stones and dropping them into a mixture of water and seeds in the basket I could make *gruel*.

9. Yet the more I thought about it, the greater my *determination* to try, for there was nothing to be found on the island that made such good spear points as the tusk-like teeth of the bull sea elephant.

Part II: Determining the Meaning   Match the vocabulary words to their dictionary definitions.

___ 28. sandspit   A. thin, cooked cereal
___ 29. pitch   B. chewed
___ 30. omen   C. uproar
___ 31. chafing   D. salty
___ 32. brackish   E. rubbing
___ 33. clamor   F. sign; indication
___ 34. gnawed   G. black sticky tar or asphalt found along beaches
___ 35. gruel   H. long, narrow shoal extending from the shore
___ 36. determination   I. conviction

Vocabulary - *Island of the Blue Dolphins* Chapters 13-15

Part I: Using Prior Knowledge and Contextual Clues
Below are the sentences in which the vocabulary words appear in the text. Read the sentence. Use any clues you can find in the sentence combined with your prior knowledge, and write what you think the underlined words mean on the lines provided.

1. Since no cows were playing among the waves in front of him, I knew that he did not have a herd of his own, and for that reason would not be so *wary* or quickly angered.

2. Quickly he overtook his *rival* and with a single thrust of his shoulders overturned him.

3. The young bull stood as high as a tall man and was twice that length, yet from the force of the blow he rolled into the water and lay there *stunned*.

4. By this time the old bull had whirled around and turned upon his *pursuer* so fast that the young bull was taken by surprise.

5. The spring was not far off and I rested there, though I was very thirsty, cutting a *lobe* from a cactus bush to chew on.

6. Far back in a corner was the half-eaten *carcass* of a fox.

Part II: Determining the Meaning   Match the vocabulary words to their dictionary definitions.

___ 37. wary   A. hunter; tracker
___ 38. rival   B. round, leafy projection
___ 39. stunned   C. cautious
___ 40. pursuer   D. dead body of an animal
___ 41. carcass   E. shocked; dazed
___ 42. lobe   F. opponent

Vocabulary *Island of the Blue Dolphins* Chapters 16-18

Part I: Using Prior Knowledge and Contextual Clues
Below are the sentences in which the vocabulary words appear in the text. Read the sentence. Use any clues you can find in the sentence combined with your prior knowledge, and write what you think the underlined words mean.

1. At that moment, while he lay there on the grass with the dog circling *warily* and the pack moving slowly toward him, without knowing that I did so, I fitted an arrow to the bow.

2. I thought it was a *lure* and so it proved to be, for suddenly they ran toward him.

3. A pair of these birds made a nest in a *stunted* tree near my house.

4. After the Aleuts had killed our men at Coral Cove, all the women of our tribe had *singed* their hair as a sign of mourning.

5. I had singed mine too, with a *faggot*, but now it had grown long again and came to my waist.

Part II: Determining the Meaning   Match the vocabulary words to their dictionary definitions.

___ 43. warily   A. shortened

___ 44. lure   B. bundle of sticks used for fuel

___ 45. stunted   C. cautiously

___ 46. singed   D. trap

___ 47. faggot   E. burnt; scorched

Vocabulary Island of the Blue Dolphins Chapters 19-21

Part I: Using Prior Knowledge and Contextual Clues

Below are the sentences in which the vocabulary words appear in the text. Read the sentence. Use any clues you can find in the sentence combined with your prior knowledge, and write what you think the underlined words mean.

1. My grip on it broke, and aware that I had struck the devilfish, I quickly dropped the coils I held, for when the string runs out fast it burns your hands or becomes *entangled*.

2. So many of his arms were *flailing* that it was useless to cut any one of them.

3. "Rontu," I said, feeling *giddy* with happiness, "if you were not a male dog I would make you one too, as beautiful as this."

Part II: Determining the Meaning   Match the vocabulary words to their dictionary definitions.

___ 48. entangled   A. silly

___ 49. flailing   B. twisted

___ 50. giddy   C. thrashing

Vocabulary - *Island of the Blue Dolphins*   Chapters 22-25

Part I: Using Prior Knowledge and Contextual Clues

Below are the sentences in which the vocabulary words appear in the text. Read the sentence. Use any clues you can find in the sentence combined with your prior knowledge, and write what you think the underlined words mean on the lines provided.

1. I worked five nights on the *circlet* and on the fifth day when she came I gave it to her, putting it around her head and tying it in the back.

2. The Aleut ship with its red-beaked *prow* and red sails had gone.

3. When he found that was all I had he swam around in circles, looking at me *reproachfully*.

Part II: Determining the Meaning   Match the vocabulary words to their dictionary definitions.

___ 51. circlet   A. with disapproval

___ 52. prow   B. ring-shaped ornament

___ 53. reproachfully   C. front end; bow

Vocabulary - *Island of the Blue Dolphins* Chapters 26-29

Part I: Using Prior Knowledge and Contextual Clues

Below are the sentences in which the vocabulary words appear in the text. Read the sentence. Use any clues you can find in the sentence combined with your prior knowledge, and write what you think the underlined words mean on the lines provided.

1., 2. Slowly the second wave forced the first one backward, rolled slowly over it, and then as a *victor* drags the *vanquished*, moved in toward the island.

3. I therefore I set out on the first fair morning to search for whatever *wreckage* the waves had washed ashore.

Part II: Determining the Meaning   Match the vocabulary words to their dictionary definitions.

___ 54. victor   A. winner
___ 55. vanquished   B. defeated
___ 56. wreckage   C. ruins

ANSWER KEY: VOCABULARY
Island of the Blue Dolphins

Author's Note

Ch.1-3	Ch. 4-7	Ch. 8,9	Ch.10-12
1. F	12. B	20. G	28. H
2. D	13. E	21. F	29. G
3. J	14. G	22. A	30. F
4. C	15. A	23. D	31. E
5. G	16. D	24. E	32. D
6. H	17. F	25. B	33. C
7. A	18. H	26. H	34. B
8. I	19. C	27. C	35. A
9. F			36. I
10. B			
11. K			

Ch. 13-15	Ch. 16-18	Ch. 19-21	Ch. 22-25	Ch.26-29
37. C	43. C	48. B	51. B	54. A
39. F	44. D	49. C	52. C	55. B
40. E	45. A	50. A	53. A	56. C
41. A	46. E			
42. D	47. B			

DAILY LESSONS

LESSON ONE

Objectives
1. To introduce *Island of the Blue Dolphins* unit
2. To give students some background information on *Island of the Blue Dolphins*
3. To distribute books and other related materials: study guides, reading assignments, etc.
4. To model effective oral reading skills by reading aloud Author's Note and Chapter 1.
5. To have students identify setting and point of view

Activity #1

Ask the class if anyone has ever been to California? Have them point out on a map where and tell about it. If anyone has been to any, this could lead into the discussion of missions on the coast of California. Be sure to point out the major cities of Los Angeles and San Diego. Show the class a map of the southern coast of California and its surrounding islands. Point out the island of San Nicolas. Tell them Scott O'Dell, the author, grew up on an island very similar to and near this island. He came across this true account while researching the history of California which forms the basis for the novel they are about to read. Ask students to listen carefully while you read the Author's Note.

Activity #2

Distribute the materials students will use in this unit. Explain in detail how students are to use these materials.

Study Guides Students should preview the study guide questions before each reading assignment to get a feeling for what events and ideas are important in that section. After reading the section, students will (as a class or individually) answer the questions to review the important events and ideas from that section of the book. Students should keep the study guides as study materials for the unit test.

Vocabulary Prior to reading a reading assignment, students will do vocabulary work related to the section of the book they are about to read. Following the completion of the reading of the book, there will be a vocabulary review of all the words used in the vocabulary assignments. Students should keep their vocabulary work as study materials for the unit test.

Reading Assignment Sheet You need to fill in the reading assignment sheet to let students know when their reading has to be completed. You can either write the assignment sheet on a side blackboard or bulletin board and leave it there for students to see each day, or you can make copies for each student to have. In either case, you should advise students to become very familiar with the reading assignments so they know what is expected of them.

Extra Activities Center The resource portions of this unit contain suggestions for a library of related books and articles in your classroom as well as crossword and word search puzzles. Make an extra activities center in your room where you will keep these materials for students to use. (Bring the books and articles in from the library and keep several copies of the puzzles on hand.) Explain to students that these materials are available for students to use when they finish reading assignments or other class work early

Books Each school has its own rules and regulations regarding student use of school books. Advise students of the procedures that are normal for your school.

Activity #3

      Have students examine the cover of the book and turn to page 1. Read this chapter to them as they follow along. Identify the use of first person narration. Encourage students to close their eyes and try to visualize the sea scene while you read. Discuss the conflict presented in this chapter and predict possible outcomes.   Assign P, V, R for Chapters 1- 3.

LESSON TWO

Objectives
1. To review the main ideas and vocabulary from Author's Note and Chapters 1-3
2. To preview study questions and vocabulary from Chapters 4-7
3. To give students the opportunity to express personal ideas in writing

Activity #1

Review the vocabulary from Author's Note and Chapters 1-3 by reproducing the matching section on the chalkboard or on an overhead transparency. Have students volunteer to come up and find the correct match for each vocabulary word. After they have made the match, ask them to use the word in an original sentence. Also have them identify its part of speech.

Activity #2

Discuss the answers to the study questions for these chapters in detail. Write the answers on the board or overhead transparency so students can have the correct answers for study purposes. Note: It is a good practice in public speaking and leadership skills for individual students to take charge of leading the discussions of the study questions. Perhaps a different student could go to the front of the class and lead the discussion each day that the study questions are discussed during this unit. Of course, the teacher should guide the discussion when appropriate and be sure to fill in any gaps the students leave.

Activity #3

Distribute Writing Assignment #1. Discuss the directions in detail. Inform students that the diaries will be collected at the end of the unit. (Give date.) Allow students time now to begin their first entry responding to their first reading assignment.

Activity #4

Give students the remaining class time to preview the study questions for Chapters 4-7 and to do the related vocabulary work. If time allows, begin reading Chapters 4-7 or assign the reading of it to be completed prior to the next class session.

WRITING ASSIGNMENT #1 - *Island of the Blue Dolphins*

PROMPT

You are going to read a story about a young Native American girl who is stranded on an isolated tropical island. Through the course of the novel, Karana develops into a character of great courage and self-reliance. The choices she makes and carries out in her day-to day survival are quite worthy of your comment.

Your assignment is to keep a diary during the time we are reading this novel. Each entry must be at least eight to ten sentences long. You may make your entries longer if you wish. You must have at least one entry for each reading assignment. (A total of 9 entries is the minimum requirement.)

PREWRITING

What will you write about? After your reading assignment has been completed, go back and review the events in it. Respond to Karana's thoughts, plans, and actions. Respond to the abundant descriptions of sea life and sea environment. What would you have done if you would have been Karana? Would you have done things differently ? in what ways? How would you have felt in her situation? What have you learned about her tribe? her environment? her intelligence? her values? What forms of sea life do you find most fascinating? What aspects of her environment do you find appealing, less than appealing? Include anything else you find interesting.

DRAFTING

What is important is that you sit down and write after each reading assignment or even more frequently. Diaries are not formal, written papers; they are a form of personal expression. There is no right or wrong thing to include in your diary. There is no formal structure- just take the time to get comfortable and let the ideas flow.

PROOFREADING

It can be quite a self-revealing exercise to go back and reread your earlier entries- not so much for proofreading purposes but to re-evaluate yourself and your feelings. One of the best ways to get to know yourself is to keep a diary or journal. We are all too frequently rushing here and there, with fleeting thoughts coming and going like wisps of smoke. It can be very helpful to slow down at some point, and record your thoughts and feelings for the day. Hopefully, this will not be the last diary you will ever write.

LESSON THREE

Objectives
1. To review the vocabulary and main events from Chapters 4-7
2. To define and identify conflict
3. To preview study questions and prereading vocabulary work for Chapters 8 and 9

Activity #1

Review the vocabulary from chapters 4-7 by asking students to practice using the vocabulary in sentences of their own with a partner. After the practice, use the matching section of the prereading vocabulary sheet for chapters 4-7 as a quiz.

Activity #2

Discuss the answers to the study guide questions for these chapters.

Activity #3

Lead students in a discussion of the term *conflict*. What do they think of when they hear the word? Have them share examples of conflict in their lives; their family's; the world; etc. Have students come up with the various types of conflict that can exist. (Man vs. Man, Man vs. Nature, Man vs. Self, etc.) Write these types on the board or overhead. After they have listed the different types, in pairs have them locate examples of these forms of conflict from chapters 4-7. List under matching heading on the board or overhead. After they have identified the examples of conflict, discuss how it was resolved in each case or predict how it will be resolved. Have students copy info from the board for their notes.

Type of Conflict	**Specific Example**	**Resolution**

Activity #4

In the remaining class time, have students do the prereading vocabulary work and preview study questions from chapters 8 and 9. If no time remains, assign this for homework.

LESSON FOUR

Objectives
1. To review the main events and vocabulary from Chapters 8 and 9
2. To preview the study questions for Chapters 10-12
3. To familiarize students with the vocabulary in Chapters 10-12
4. To make predictions

Activity #1
Review the vocabulary from chapters 8 and 9 by dividing the class into small groups. Have students quickly copy the vocabulary words onto blank cards. Next, have them copy the definitions onto separate cards. Turn all the cards over, after mixing them up. Have students take turns flipping two cards over to determine if they are a match. If they are a match, that person gets to keep that pair and gets another turn. Students may look at the vocabulary words in their contextual sentences for help, if needed. Continue play until all words are matched with their definitions. If they are ready for a further challenge, add vocabulary from previous chapters. This is similar to the game Concentration.

Activity #2
Use the multiple choice format of the study guide questions for chapters 8 and 9 as a quiz to check that students have done the required reading and to review the main ideas of chapters 8 and 9. Exchange papers for checking and discuss answers.

Activity #3
Give students about ten minutes to do the prereading vocabulary work and preview study questions from chapters 10-12. After they have done this, ask them to make at least two predictions of what is going to happen in the next three chapters. Have them put these away until after they have read the assigned reading of chapters 10-12.

LESSON FIVE

Objectives
1. To review the vocabulary and main events and ideas from Chapters 10-12
2. To recognize, define and practice the process of decision making
3. To encourage required diary writing

Activity #1

Have students retrieve their earlier predictions. Were they accurate? Perhaps you may want to reward those students who were accurate with some small prize. Discuss the answers to the study questions for chapters 10-12 in this manner. Make a copy of the study guide questions with answers and the matching vocabulary section. Cut them apart, separating the questions and answers or vocabulary word and definition into two piles. Divide the class into two teams. Give one team the questions (or vocab word) ; the other team the answers (or definition). Divide them up among the players so only one person has one question or answer. Select one team to begin play. One person from that team reads one of the questions or answers. Next, a member from the other team tries to match up with the corresponding response. When it is a correct match, move on to another question. Continue play until all questions are answered correctly.

Activity #2

Living alone on the island has forced Karana to make many decisions. She practices sound judgment and reason when considering her options and choices. Divide the class into small groups. Assign each group a chapter to review for examples of the problems Karana faces, and her methods of solving them. After each group has finished, have them share their findings with the class. Encourage note-taking for further reference.

Activity #3

Using the following form, have each small group come up with a problem they are or have been faced with. Have them problem solve together and then share their decisions with the group.

Activity #4

Give students the remaining class time to add to their personal diaries.

DECISION-MAKING MODEL

PROBLEM

POSSIBLE OBSTACLES

POSSIBLE SOLUTIONS

Solution A	+	−

Solution B	+	−

Solution C	+	−

DECISION

LESSON SIX

Objectives
1. To preview prereading vocabulary work and study guide questions for Chapters 13-15
2. To give students practice in writing to persuade
3. To discuss Project Travel Poster and Brochure

Activity #1

In pairs, have students preview prereading vocabulary and study guide questions for chapters 13-15. Assign reading of these chapters as homework in preparation for the next class session.

Activity #2

Distribute Writing Assignment #2. Discuss the directions in detail. Give them a specific due date. (Conference will be held during Lesson 9 class time.) Tell them the following project supports this writing activity ; they go hand in hand.

Activity #3

Acquaint your class with the independent project. Discuss directions thoroughly and give students due date. (Project sharing is scheduled for Lesson #16) It is a good idea to give students *specific* criteria to meet a *specific* grade as presented in Activity #3 below.

WRITING ASSIGNMENT #2 - *Island of the Blue Dolphins*

PROMPT

During the course of your reading of *Island of the Blue Dolphins*, you have been exposed to a variety of detailed descriptions of Karana's island. Is the tropical climate and sealife of this location appealing to you? Many folks spend vacations in climates similar to this. Where would you most like to spend your next vacation? Your goal is to prepare a letter to your parents or guardians convincing them to take you to the location of your choice for your next vacation.

PREWRITING

The first thing you need to do is to decide where it is that you would like to go. You probably have an idea of someplace that appeals to you from reading, movies, or other sources. Do some research to determine your final choice. To begin with, create a list of facts, opinions, and examples that support your choice of location.. Come up with any and all possible arguments you can think of that will promote your choice in this matter. Decide which are your strongest justifiable arguments, and which are less substantial. Organize your points from weaker to strongest utilizing your facts, opinions, and examples as evidence in support of your argument.

DRAFTING

Begin with an introductory paragraph in which you express your desire to visit the location of your choice. Follow that with one paragraph for each of the main points you have to support your argument to convince your parents or guardians that this is the vacation you've all been waiting for. Fill in each paragraph with your facts, opinions, and examples that support your decision. Then, write an ending paragraph that summarizes and restates your intention to vacation in this location as your final statement.

PROMPT

When you finish the rough draft of your paper, ask a student who sits near you to read it. After reading your rough draft, he\she should tell you what he\she liked best about your work, which parts were difficult to understand, and ways in which your work could be improved. Reread your paper considering your critic's comments, and make the corrections you think are necessary.

PROOFREADING

Do a final proofreading of your paper double-checking your grammar, spelling, organization, and the clarity of your ideas.

PROJECT TRAVEL POSTER AND BROCHURE
Island of the Blue Dolphins

Objectives:

Project Travel Poster and Brochure is a project included in this unit as a support for Writing Assignment #2. Students will work on this independently on their own time outside of class. If so inclined, you may choose to change these requirements to meet your specific students' needs. It seems the perfect time to allow students creative license to create a travel poster and brochure advertising their ideal vacation spot to further promote their choice.

Activity #1

Tell students that once they have decided upon their ideal vacation location for Writing Assignment#2, they need to collect as much specific information describing this place as possible. Brainstorm all imaginable sources of information such as: almanacs, travel guides, travel agencies, encyclopedias, computer software, etc.

Activity #2

After students have compiled a list of sources they are willing to use, have them brainstorm ideas for the topics they need to cover in their research. Possible subtopics might include: climate, animal life, language, food, recreation, entertainment, transportation, historical value, tours, etc.

Activity #3

Perhaps you could schedule them into the school library to do the actual research or encourage independent research at this point. Remind them that their final goal is to represent their findings in an appealing visual form through a poster and brochure. It would be a good idea to display a sample of the size and quality that you are expecting. Outline specific requirements regarding print size, medium to be used, etc. Perhaps you could allow class input in this part. The more input students have, the more cooperative and willing they will be to put out the effort. You could display a variety of commercial examples as models too. Have fun!

LESSON SEVEN

Objectives
1. To review the main events and ideas from Chapters 13-15
2. To preview the vocabulary and study guide questions for Chapters 16-18
3. To give students practice in oral reading
4. To provide students with the opportunity to write in their diaries

Activity #1

Use the multiple choice format of the study guide questions for chapters 13-15 as a quiz to check that students have done the required reading and to review the main ideas of chapters 13-15. Exchange papers for checking and discuss answers.

Activity #2

In small groups, have students preview prereading vocabulary and study guide questions for chapters 16-18.

Activity #3

Have students read chapters 13-15 aloud in class. You probably know the best way to motivate oral reading in your class; pick students at random, ask for volunteers, have student who already read choose the next one, spin a spinner that designates students, or whatever works for you.

Activity #4

Give students remaining class time to continue responding in their diaries.

LESSON EIGHT

Objectives
    1. To review the main events and ideas from Chapters 16-18
    2. To discuss the theme of survival
    3. To identify traits necessary for survival

Activity #1

    Hand out four little slips of paper or mini cards to each student that have the letters A,B,C, or D on them. A good idea is to use different color cards for each letter. Use the multiple choice study guide questions and answers on chapters 16-18 for an oral review. Read the question (and/ or show it on the overhead). Then give students the four possible answers, labeling them A, B, C, or D (or show on overhead again). Students respond by holding up the card with what they think is the correct answer. This is one variety of Every Student Response. Remind students not to look at what others are holding up, but to simply display the card of their choice. This is a quick indicator of students' comprehension. You can make it somewhat different by requiring complete silence and having them read the questions silently from the overhead, or make it more mysterious (fun?) by blindfolding everyone and have them hold up a certain number of fingers per answer instead of using the cards.

Activity #2

    In small groups have students brainstorm character traits Karana displays that allow her to survive as well as she does. After students have determined the necessary traits, place each of them in the center of a separate web on the chalkboard. List specific actions and behaviors of Karana that can be attributed to each trait on lines extending from each web. Allow full class participation and encourage note-taking.

Activity #3

    Returning to their small groups, have students discuss how they think they would have managed to survive in Karana's place. Have them determine what would have been their greatest obstacle; their least difficult obstacle. Share findings with the entire class.

NOTE: Explain to students that you will be having writing conferences in the next class session. During the writing conference, you will discuss their writing skills individually, based on their second writing assignment in this unit.

LESSON NINE

Objectives
1. To do the prereading vocabulary work for Chapters 19-21
2. To preview study guide questions for Chapters 19-21
3. To silently read Chapters 19-21
4. To evaluate students' writing
5. To have students revise their Writing Assignment 2 papers

Activity #1
   Assign the prereading vocabulary pages, study guide questions and silent reading of chapters 19-21. Students should work on this independently while they are waiting for their conference with you.

Activity #2
   Call students to your desk (or some other private area) to discuss their papers from Writing Assignment #2. Use the following Writing Evaluation Form to help structure your conference. Give students a date when their revisions are due. (They will be sharing these along with their projects in Lesson #16.)

WRITING EVALUATION FORM - *Island of the Blue Dolphins*

Name _____ Date _____

Writing Assignment #1 for *Island of the Blue Dolphins* unit   Grade _____

Circle One For Each Item:

Description (paragraph 1)	excellent	good	fair	poor
Plans (body paragraphs)	excellent	workable	fair	not realistic
Conclusion	excellent	good	fair	poor
Grammar:	excellent	good	fair	poor (errors noted)
Spelling:	excellent	good	fair	poor (errors noted)
Punctuation:	excellent	good	fair	poor (errors noted)
Legibility:	excellent	good	fair	poor

Strengths:

Weaknesses:

Comments/Suggestions:

LESSON TEN

<u>Objectives</u>
1. To introduce simile, personification, and metaphor as figures of speech
2. To distinguish between three different types of figurative language/ literary devices
3. To have students locate figurative language in the text
4. To create original figures of speech
5. To illustrate figurative language

<u>Activity #1</u>
      Tell the class you are going to read a few sentences to them from their most recently read chapters in the book. Ask them to listen carefully and try to identify similarities between them or see if they can identify what they are examples of:

    -They are as hard to pry loose from an abalone as an abalone is to pry from a rock.
    -Scallops fell on the reef like rain.
    -One struck me on the leg and burned like a whip.
    -The head rose out of the twisting arms like a giant stalk.
    -The sound echoed through the cave like the howling of a whole pack of dogs.
    -As the water lapped against the wall it sounded like the soft music of a flute.
    -The skirt flowed around her like water.

These examples all happen to be similes. Point out the use of *like* and *as* to create the comparisons. When ready, move on the Activity #2

<u>Activity #2</u>
      Make three columns on the chalkboard labeling each one separately: simile, metaphor, and personification. Spend some time here instructing about the other two forms of figurative language. You could use specific examples from the following test, focusing on the ones from earlier chapters. Perhaps you could cite some examples from familiar songs. Ask why they think any author or lyricist would use them? Do they use them? Why? In what way does using them enhance speaking or writing or the understanding of each of these. As a whole group, have students give you examples they can think of and then have them locate a few in any part of the text they have read. Allow them to come to the board and write these under the correct heading. When you are satisfied with their ability to recognize them and differentiate between them, go to the next activity.

Activity #3

Divide the class into small groups of three or four. Have each group assign a recorder. Give them a couple of sheets of paper. Ask each group to locate as many of these figures of speech as they can from the text. They may be more successful in the portion they already have read, but it isn't necessary to limit them. Giving them a time constraint is an option. It could be a race, you are the judge. You may want to rule out using the ones that are posted on the board. It's up to you. There are an endless supply in every chapter. Wrap this activity up by having the group with the **most** read their list aloud. Decide as a whole group if indeed each one is correct. Have all groups check off the ones that are read that they also found. Allow every group to read any that have not yet been mentioned. You could give small treats for first, second, third place, etc.

Activity #4

Have students create one example of each type. They could be individual sentences or you could require them to write a short paragraph using all three. Base this on the ability level of your students and/or time. Create one together as a model. If time, have them illustrate it with original art work or magazine pictures. Save finished products for display. They could do this part as homework.

NOTE: The following figurative language test is optional. You may want to use it right after instruction, later in this unit, or not at all. You may choose to use it only as a resource for this lesson. It contains examples from the entire book.

FIGURATIVE LANGUAGE TEST - *Island of the Blue Dolphins*

I. Read the following examples of figurative language. Label each one separately with either an **S** for simile, **P** for personification, or an **M** for metaphor.

1. Then it grew larger and was a gull with folded wings. _____
2. He was small for one who had lived so many suns and moons, but quick as a cricket. _____
3. "The sea is smooth, it is a flat stone without any scratches." _____
4. "To me it is a blue stone." _____
5. "In the morning when he crawls out he sits on a rock and combs until the beard shines like a cormorant's wing. _____
6. He had small eyes like the the edge of a stone knife. _____
7. They broke against the rocks and roared into the caves. _____
8. As Ulape and I ran along the cliff a whirring sound like a great bird in flight passed above our heads. _____
9. The huts looked like ghosts in the cold light. _____
10. I followed them across two hills and a small valley to a third hill whose face was a ledge of rock. _____
11. The early morning sun shone like gold on their glossy pelts. _____
12. The canoe made a path in the black water like a snake. _____
13. The fog crept in and out of the empty huts. _____
14. The noise of the surf was their voices speaking. _____
15. In front of me lay the dim line of the island like a great fish sunning itself on the sea. _____
16. Like gray boulders the bulls sat on the pebbly slope. _____
17. He went over them as if they were small stones. _____
18. The tongues of water licked into all the crevices, dragged at my hand and at my bare feet gripping the ledge.. _____
19. Pelicans were chattering as they fished the water. _____
20. A pup came slowly toward me, a round ball of fur that I could have held in my hand. _____

II. List one example of your own for each type of figurative language. They can be original or from your favorite songs or poetry.

III. Illustrate your favorite example of figurative language from those listed. (Use the back of this page.)

ANSWER KEY- FIGURATIVE LANGUAGE TEST
Island of the Blue Dolphins

I.
1. M
2. S
3. M
4. M
5. S
6. S
7. P
8. S
9. S
10. M
11. S
12. S
13. P
14. M
15. S
16. S
17. S
18. P
19. P
20. M

LESSON ELEVEN

Objective
1. To review vocabulary from chapters 13-21
2. To reinforce main ideas and events from chapters 19-21
3. To discuss the theme of companionship

Activity #1

Have students pair up. Using easels (if available) or scrap/drawing paper, one student draws an impression of one of the vocabulary words, while the other person tries to guess which word it is. After identifying correctly, students need to use word in an original sentence. Now student who answered earlier does the drawing. Continue play until all vocabulary from chapters 13-21 have been covered. Students may use he top section of their prereading vocabulary sheets as a resource for this activity. This is similar to the game Pictionary.

Activity #2

Divide the class into two teams. Play a game like a spelling bee, but instead of spelling a word, they must answer one of the study guide questions correctly Using the study guide questions from chapters 19-21, begin play. 1. Determine which team goes first. 2. Read one of the questions for one team member to answer. 3. If it was answered correctly, that team gets a point. 4. If it was not answered correctly, the other team gets a try at the same question. 5. Question goes back and forth until it is answered correctly. 6. Read another question, and repeat earlier play. 7. Continue play until all questions from chapters 19-21 have been covered. 8. Reward winning team with some small prize or other incentive.

Activity #3

Show pictures of examples of activities someone is enjoying with a companion. Be sure to include a variety of activities with a variety of companions: pets, older people, peers, etc. Ask students what they think all the pictures share. Lead them to coming up with the word *companionship*. Allow students to define their concept of this word. Next, have them share examples of the types of companionship they seek and enjoy. Discuss Karana's need for this and how she coped with it. It time, have students sketch scenes from the book that depict Karana's various companions and their role in her existence.

Activity #4

Assign PVR for chapters 22-25 as homework to be completed by the next class session.

LESSON TWELVE

Objectives
    1. To review the vocabulary and main ideas and events from chapters 22-25
    2. To give students practice reading orally
    3. To evaluate students' oral reading

Activity #1

    Have students glance over the vocabulary from Chapters 22-29. Write each of the six words separately on the chalkboard leaving space beneath each one, or on separate pieces of newsprint taped to the wall around the room. Divide the class into six teams or pairs.. Have each team list as many synonyms for their word as they can come up with, beneath it, on the chalkboard or newsprint. Give them a time limit and reward the team who comes up with the most correct synonyms. It is up to you if you want them to be able to refer to a thesaurus or dictionary first. If class can handle, you could have them give an at least one antonym for their word too.

Activity #2

    Review the main ideas and events from Chapters 22-25 allowing your class to decide in which manner they would like to do that. They could choose from any of the earlier techniques, or devise a new one.

Activity #3

    Have students read chapters 26-29 orally in class. You probably know the best way to get readers within your class; pick students at random, ask for volunteers, have students who have just read select another student, assign numbers to students and spin a spinner, or whatever works best for you. Complete the oral reading evaluation form that follows this lesson after listening to your students read.

ORAL READING EVALUATION - *Island of the Blue Dolphins*

Name _____ Class____ Date _____

SKILL	EXCELLENT	GOOD	AVERAGE	FAIR	POOR
Fluency	5	4	3	2	1
Clarity	5	4	3	2	1
Audibility	5	4	3	2	1
Pronunciation	5	4	3	2	1
_____	5	4	3	2	1
_____	5	4	3	2	1

Total _____ Grade _____

Comments:

LESSONS THIRTEEN AND FOURTEEN

Objectives:
1. To discuss the ideas and themes from *Island of the Blue Dolphins* in greater detail
2. To have students exercise their interpretive and critical thinking skills
3. To relate some of the ideas in *Island of the Blue Dolphins* to the students' lives

Activity #1

Choose the questions from the Extra Discussion Questions/Writing Assignments which seem most appropriate for your students. A class discussion of these questions is most effective if students have been given the opportunity to formulate answers to the questions prior to the discussion. To this end, you may either have all the students formulate answers to all the questions, divide your class into groups and assign one or more questions to each group, or you could assign one question to each student in your class. The option you choose will make a difference in the amount of class time needed for this activity.

Activity #2

After students have had ample time to formulate answers to the questions, begin your class discussion of the questions and the ideas presented by the questions. Be sure students take notes during the discussion so they have information to study for the unit test.

EXTRA DISCUSSION QUESTIONS/WRITING ASSIGNMENTS
Island of the Blue Dolphins

Interpretive
1. From whose point of view is the story written? How does it affect us as we read it?

2. Identify the setting and tell how it shapes this story.

3. What are the *primary* challenges Karana faces and how does she meet them?

4. Define foreshadowing. Give examples of foreshadowing used in *Island of the Blue Dolphins*.

5. Where does the climax occur in this novel? Support your choice.

6. How were the Aleuts portrayed by the author?

7. Is this story believable? Explain your answer.

8. After reading some biographical information on Scott O'Dell, defend his choice of setting and his stand on animals in this particular novel.

9. What do the dolphins represent to Karana as she leaves with the white men?

10. Complete a character analysis for Karana.

11. If Karana admires the beads and bracelets in the chest so greatly, why does she fling them into the sea?

Critical
12. Some of the *very* things Karana fears will happen if she makes and uses weapons, happen during the course of the book. Translate O'Dell's reasons for including them.

13. Explain the significance of the Aleut ship's red sails; the other ships's white sails.

14. How would the story have changed if Ramo had not been killed?

15. For what reason did O'Dell use Karana's secret name throughout the novel rather than her common name of Won-a-pa-lei?

16. How could Karana ultimately save and befriend Rontu when he was the dog who killed Ramo?

Island of the Blue Dolphins Extra Discussion Questions page 2

17. Justify the author's decision to base this survival story on a *young woman* rather than a *young man*.

18. Contrast Karana's state of mind *before* and *after* her attempted canoe trip (p.60-67).

19. Characterize Scott O'Dell's writing style. How does it complement the content of the novel?

20. Explain Karana's statement "Now that the white man had come back, I could not think of what I would do when I went across the sea, or make a picture in my mind of the white men and what they did there, or see my people who had been gone so long. Nor, thinking of the past, of the many summers and winters and springs that had gone, could I see each of them. They were all one, a tight feeling in my breast and nothing more.

Critical/ Personal Response

21. What *else* could Karana have done when Matasaip would not turn the ship around for Ramo? Do you think the ship would have returned soon enough to save Ramo? When have you acted against an adult's direction because it was the right thing for you to do?

22. Why is Karana puzzled when her father gives his secret name to the Russian? Can you identify with a time you questioned your parent's judgment, silently or not-so-silently?

23. Is Karana resourceful? Why or why not? Share your resourcefulness.

24. Why is Karana compelled to rescue and nurse the wounded otter she finds after the Aleuts leave? Share a time you or someone else found and/or nursed an injured animal.

25. What does Karana learn about herself through this experience? How do you think it influences her life at the Santa Barbara Mission? Have you ever found yourself in a challenging situation that helped you learn more about who you are?

Personal Response

26. How would *you* have fared if you had been in Karana's situation? What character traits do you have that would have been strengths? weaknesses?

27. After despising him and plotting to kill him, Karana comes to value and love Rontu. Have you ever seen someone in a different light which caused you to change your attitude toward them?

28. Karana relies on the familiar to make explanations. She describes her island as if it were a dolphin. Using a familiar (known to them) reference, describe (unknown to them) something to someone.

Island of the Blue Dolphins Extra Discussion Questions page 3

29. It took much trial and error for Karana to fashion a useful bow and arrow because she had watched her father make weapons, but not with the eye of one who would ever do it. Describe how this situation applies to you. What conclusion about *learning* can you draw from these examples?

30. After Rontu's hard-won victory with the wild dogs, he walked to the top of the mound and lifted his head and gave a long howl. Karana had never heard the sound before and did not understand it. How would you interpret Rontu's behavior?

31. Karana takes only three baskets, her dog, and cage of birds with her for her new life. What would be the most important things for you to take with you if you were to relocate? Explain.

Quotations
1. "The sea is smooth. I think it is a flat, blue stone without any scratches. And far away on the edge of it is a small cloud which sits on the stone."

2. "I am the Chief of Ghalas-at, my name is Chief Chowig."

3. "I have come in peace and wish to parley. We come to hunt sea otter. We wish to camp on your island while we are hunting."

4. "The sea which surrounds the Island of the Blue Dolphins belongs to us."

5. "The parts shall be equal."

6. "Their ways are not ours nor is their language. They are people who do not understand friendship."

7. "In the morning when he crawls out of his tent he sits on a rock and combs until the beard shines like a cormorant's wing."

8. "She is dressed in skins just like the men, but she wears a fur cap and under the cap she has thick hair that falls to her waist."

9. "A school of white bass. On the rocks. A dozen of them. Perhaps more than a dozen."

10. "You have fish. You can spare two. We tire of the dried ones. Captain Orlov will hear of that you refuse to share the fish."

Island of the Blue Dolphins Extra Discussion Questions page 4

11. "Go and hunt your own fish. I have my people to think of."

12. "There are scarcely a dozen otter left in the beds around Coral Cove. Before the Aleuts came there were many."

13. "One string of beads for one otter pelt is not our bargain. The rest of the pelts must stay here until the chests are brought."

14. "Most of those who snared fowl and found fish in the deep water and built canoes are gone. The women, who were never asked to do more than stay at home, cook food, and make clothing, now must take the place of the men and face the dangers which abound beyond the village."

15. "The ship does not belong to our enemies, the Aleuts. There are white men on this ship and they have come from that place where Kimki went when he left our island. The ship has come for one reason, to take us away from Ghalas-at.

16. "We cannot wait for Ramo, if we do the ship will be driven on the rocks. The ship will come back for him on another day."

17. "I do not care if the ship never comes. Tomorrow I am going to where the canoes are hidden and bring one back to Coral Cove. We will use it to fish and go looking around the island."

18. "But first you must become a man. As it is the custom, therefore, I will have to whip you with a switch of nettles and then tie you to a red-ant hill."

19. "I have thought of a name. I am Chief Tanyositlopai."

20. "I vowed that someday I would go back and kill the wild dogs in the cave. I would kill all of them. I thought of how I would do it, but mostly I thought of Ramo, my brother."

21. "As I lay there I wondered what would happen to me if I went against the laws of our tribe which forbade the making of weapons by women. Would the four winds blow in from the four directions of the world and smother me as I made the weapons? Or would the earth tremble, as many said and bury me beneath its falling rock? Or as others said, would the sea rise over the island in a terrible flood? Would the weapons break in my hands at the moment when my life was in danger, which is what my father said?"

Island of the Blue Dolphins Extra Discussion Questions page 5

22. "I had decided during the days of the storm, when I had given up hope of seeing the ship, that I would take one of the canoes and go to the country that lay toward the east. I must say that whatever might befall me on the endless waters did not trouble me. It meant far less than the thought of staying on the island alone."

23. "Dolphins are animals of good omen. It made me happy to have them swimming around the canoe, now that I had friends with me I did not feel the same."

24. "I was happy to be home. Everything that I saw filled me with happiness."

25. "How could I possibly kill one of those great beasts? The more I thought about it, the greater was my determination to try, for there was nothing to be found on the island that made such good spear points as the tusklike teeth of the bull sea elephant."

26. "Dog, Dog. He looked first at the fish I carried and then at me and moved his tail. I named him Rontu, which means in our language Fox Eyes."

27. "Rontu, tell me why it is that you are such a handsome dog and yet such a thief?"

28. "I did not know how lonely I had been until I had Rontu to talk to."

29. "I also made a wreath for Rontu's neck, which he did not like. Together we would walk along the cliff looking at the sea, and though the white man's ship did not return that spring, it was a happy time.

30. "I saw two more giant devilfish along the reef that summer, but I did not try to spear them."

31. "Tutok. Wintscha, Wintscha. Mah-nay, Karana.

32. "I never killed another animal. This is the way I felt about the animals who had become my friends and those who were not, but in time could be. If Ulape and my father had come back and laughed, and all the others had come back and laughed, still I would have felt the same way, for animals and birds are like people too, though they do not talk the same or do the same things. Without them the earth would be an unhappy place."

33. "Until that summer, I had kept count of all the moons since the time my brother and I were alone upon the island. For each one that came and went I cut a mark in a pole beside the door of my house. There were many marks, from the roof to the floor. But after that summer I did not cut them any more."

Island of the Blue Dolphins Extra Discussion Questions page 6

34. "Rontu, you have always liked to bark at the seagulls. Whole mornings and afternoons you have barked at them. Bark at them now for me. Rontu, oh, Rontu!"

35. "There were happy times that summer, fishing and going to Tall Rock on our canoe, but more and more I thought of Tutok and my sister Ulape. Sometimes I would hear their voices in the wind and often, when I was on the sea, in the waves that lapped softly against the canoe."

36. "All night as we lay there in the house the earth trembled and rocks fell, yet not the big one on the headland, which would have fallen if those who make the world shake had really been angry with us. "

37. "I thought of many things, but stronger was the wish to be where people lived, to hear their voices and their laughter."

38. "His words made the strangest sounds I have ever heard. At first I wanted to laugh, but I bit my tongue."

39. "From time to time he would hold up the dress and nod his head as if he were pleased. I nodded as if I were pleased, too, but I was not. I wanted to wear my cormorant skirt and my otter cape, which were more beautiful than the thing he was making."

LESSON FIFTEEN

Objectives:
1. To give students practice in writing to inform
2. To give students the opportunity to fulfill their nonfiction reading assignment that goes along with this unit

Activity #1

Allow each of your students to select a topic to research that appeals to them from the Bulletin Board Ideas/ Extra Activities Section of the unit. Some topics may require a pair of students, or a small group to research. Distribute Writing Assignment #3. Discuss the directions in detail. Take your students to the library so they may work on the assignment. Students should fill out a "Nonfiction Assignment Sheet" for at least one of the sources they used, and students should submit these sheets with their compositions.

WRITING ASSIGNMENT #3 - *Island of the Blue Dolphins*

PROMPT

You have just read a story about a very courageous young girl who proves herself, despite tremendous odds. It is realistic or historical fiction (the events in the novel *could* have taken place, but the characters and events are *fictional*). Woven into this story are a variety of factual environmental issues, weather conditions, Native American traditions, animal and bird life, etc.

You have chosen one topic of interest to you about which you need to find information. You are to read as much as you can about that topic and write a composition in which you relate what you have learned from your reading. Note that this is a *composition*, not just a sentence or two.

PREWRITING

You will go to the library. When you get there, use the library's resources to find information about your topic. Look for books, encyclopedias, articles in magazines- anything that will give you the information you require. Take a few notes as you read to help you remember important dates, names, places, or other details that will be important in your composition.

After you have gathered information and become well-read on the subject of your report, make a little outline, putting your facts in order.

DRAFTING

You will need an introductory paragraph in which you introduce your topic.

In the body of your composition, put the "meat" of your research- the facts you found- in paragraph form. Each paragraph should have a topic sentence (a sentence letting the reader know what the paragraph will be about) followed by an explanation, examples or details.

Write a concluding paragraph in which you summarize the information you found and conclude your report.

PROMPT

After you have finished a rough draft of your paper, revise it yourself until you are happy with your work. Then, ask a student who sits near you to tell you what he/she likes best about your work, and what things he/she thinks can be improved. Take another look at your composition, keeping in mind your critic's suggestions, and make the revisions you feel are necessary.

PROOFREADING

Do a final proofreading of your paper double-checking your grammar, spelling, organization, and the clarity of your ideas.

NONFICTION ASSIGNMENT SHEET - *Island of the Blue Dolphins*
(To be completed after reading the required nonfiction article)

Name _____ Date _____

Title of Nonfiction Read _____

Written By _____ Publication Date _____

I. Factual Summary: Write a short summary of the piece you read.

II. Vocabulary
 1. With which vocabulary words in the piece did you encounter some degree of difficulty?

 2. How did you resolve your lack of understanding with these words?

III. Interpretation: What was the main point the author wanted you to get from reading his work?

IV. Criticism
 1. With which points of the piece did you agree or find easy to accept? Why?

 2. With which points of the piece did you disagree or find difficult to believe? Why?

V. Personal Response: What do you think about this piece? <u>OR</u> How does this piece influence your ideas.

LESSONS SIXTEEN AND SEVENTEEN

Objective:
1. To give students the opportunity to share their projects and persuasive essays
2. To give students the opportunity to share their nonfiction reading assignment

Activity #1

Invite students to share their projects with the class : travel posters and brochures. They could also read their persuasive essays on the topic of their vacation poster.

Activity #2

Allow students to share information learned from doing Writing Assignment #3 and the included nonfiction report.

LESSON EIGHTEEN

Objectives
 To review all of the vocabulary work done in this unit

Activity
 Choose one (or more) of the vocabulary review activities listed on the next page(s) and spend your class period as directed in the activity. Some of the materials for these review activities are located in the Vocabulary Resources section of this unit.

Vocabulary Review Activities

1. Divide your class into two teams and have an old-fashioned spelling or definition bee.
2. Give each of your students (or students in groups of two, three or four) a *Island of the Blue Dolphins* Vocabulary Word Search Puzzle. The person (group) to find all of the vocabulary words in the puzzle first wins.
3. Give students a *Island of the Blue Dolphins* Vocabulary Word Search Puzzle without the word list. The person or group to find the most vocabulary words in the puzzle wins.
4. Use a *Island of the Blue Dolphins* Vocabulary Crossword Puzzle. Put the puzzle onto a transparency on the overhead projector (so everyone can see it), and do the puzzle together as a class.
5. Give students a *Island of the Blue Dolphins* Vocabulary Matching Worksheet to do.
6. Divide your class into two teams. Use *Island of the Blue Dolphins* vocabulary words with their letters jumbled as a word list. Student 1 from Team A faces off against Student 1 from Team B. You write the first jumbled word on the board. The first student (1A or 1B) to unscramble the word wins the chance for his/her team to score points. If 1A wins the jumble, go to student 2A and give him/her a definition. He/she must give you the correct spelling of the vocabulary word which fits that definition. If he/she does, Team A scores a point, and you give student 3A a definition for which you expect a correctly spelled matching vocabulary word. Continue giving Team A definitions until some team member makes an incorrect response. An incorrect response sends the game back to the jumbled-word face off, this time with students 2A and 2B. Instead of repeating giving definitions to the first few students of each team, continue with the student after the one who gave the last incorrect response on the team. For example, if Team B wins the jumbled-word face-off, and student 5B gave the last incorrect answer for Team B, you would start this round of definition questions with student 6B, and so on. The team with the most points wins!
7. Have students write a story in which they correctly use as many vocabulary words as possible. Have students read their compositions orally. Post the most original compositions on your bulletin board.

LESSON NINETEEN

Objective
  To review the main ideas presented in *Island of the Blue Dolphins*

Activity #1
  Choose one of the review games/activities included in the packet and spend your class period as outlined there. Some materials for these activities are located in the Extra Activities Packet section of this unit.

Activity #2
  Remind students that the Unit Test will be in the next class meeting. Stress the review of the Study Guides and their class notes as a last minute, brush-up review for the unit test.

REVIEW GAMES/ACTIVITIES - *Island of the Blue Dolphins*

1. Ask the class to make up a unit test for *Island of the Blue Dolphins*. The test should have 4 sections: matching, true/false, short answer, and essay. Students may use 1/2 period to make the test and then swap papers and use the other 1/2 class period to take a test a classmate has devised. (open book) You may want to use the unit test included in this packet or take questions from the students' unit tests to formulate your own test.

2. Take 1/2 period for students to make up true and false questions (including the answers). Collect the papers and divide the class into two teams. Draw a big tic-tac-toe board on the chalk board. Make one team X and one team O. Ask questions to each side, giving each student one turn. If the question is answered correctly, that students' team's letter (X or O) is placed in the box. If the answer is incorrect, no mark is placed in the box. The object is to get three marks in a row like tic-tac-toe. You may want to keep track of the number of games won for each team.

3. Take 1/2 period for students to make up questions (true/false and short answer). Collect the questions. Divide the class into two teams. You'll alternate asking questions to individual members of teams A & B (like in a spelling bee). The question keeps going from A to B until it is correctly answered, then a new question is asked. A correct answer does not allow the team to get another question. Correct answers are +2 points; incorrect answers are -1 point.

4. Have students pair up and quiz each other from their study guides and class notes.

5. Give students a *Island of the Blue Dolphins* crossword puzzle to complete.

6. Divide your class into two teams. Use *Island of the Blue Dolphins* crossword words with their letters jumbled as a word list. Student 1 from Team A faces off against Student 1 from Team B. You write the first jumbled word on the board. The first student (1A or 1B) to unscramble the word wins the chance for his/her team to score points. If 1A wins the jumble, go to student 2A and give him/her a clue. He/she must give you the correct word which matches that clue. If he/she does, Team A scores a point, and you give student 3A a clue for which you expect another correct response. Continue giving Team A clues until some team member makes an incorrect response. An incorrect response sends the game back to the jumbled-word face off, this time with students 2A and 2B. Instead of repeating giving clues to the first few students of each team, continue with the student after the one who gave the last incorrect response on the team. For example, if Team B wins the jumbled-word face-off, and student 5B gave the last incorrect answer for Team B, you would start this round of clue questions with student 6B, and so on.

UNIT TESTS

SHORT ANSWER UNIT TEST #1 - *Island of the Blue Dolphins*

I. Matching/Identify

___ Sea Elephant tooth   A. Yellow-bearded Russian

___ Channel Islands   B. Wished to marry Nanko

___ Black Cave   C. Female tamed bird

___ Rontu   D. Aleut girlfriend

___ Captain Orlov   E. Dropped scallops from the sky

___ Devilfish   F. When Indians settled on island

___ Pelican   G. Needed for spear

___ Santa Barbara   H. Sea grotto with row of statues

___ Ulape   I. Yellow-eyed dog

___ Chief Chowig   J. Survived eighteen years alone

___ Lurai   K. Arms have rows of suckers

___ Tutok   L. Author

___ 2000 B.C.   M. Eight islands off coast of California

___ Karana   N. Clifornia mission

___ O'Dell   O. Karana's father

Short Answer Unit Test #1 - *Island of the Blue Dolphins* Page 2

II. Short Answer

1. Whose true story is this novel based upon?

2. For what reason had the Russian and his crew come to the island?

3. What agreement of payment was reached between the Aleuts and Karana's father, Chief Chowig?

4. Explain the otter slaughtering process as told by Karana.

5. Describe the battle between the hunters and the island warriors.

6. How does life change in Ghalas-at?

7. What does Karana do when she realizes the ship is not returning for her brother?

8. Where does Ramo go alone against Karana's instructions?

9. How does Karana end the haunting village's sights and sounds?

Short Answer Unit Test #1 - *Island of the Blue Dolphins* Page 3

10. What makes her decide to go against the tribe's law?

11. Why is it difficult for her to make the weapons?

12. In what way do Karana's feelings change when she returns to the island?

13. Describe the house she builds.

14. How is Karana able to work at night with no sunlight?

15. What warning of her father's enters Karana's mind twice while preparing her attack?

16. Why doesn't Karana shoot the wild dogs who are Rontu's rivals?

Short Answer Unit Test #1 - *Island of the Blue Dolphins* Page 4

17. How does Karana feel after Tutok leaves?

18. In what way have Karana's feelings changed about the island animals?

19. Why did Karana stop counting the moons as they passed?

20. What does Karana do to prepare to leave the island?

Short Answer Unit Test #1 - *Island of the Blue Dolphins* Page 5

III. Essay

Explain Karana's statement "Now that the white man had come back, I could not think of what I would do when I went across the sea, or make a picture in my mind of the white men and what they did there, or see my people who had been gone so long. Nor, thinking of the past, of the many summers and winters and springs that had gone, could I see each of them. They were all one, a tight feeling in my breast and nothing more.

IV. Vocabulary

Listen to the vocabulary words and spell them. After you have spelled all the words, go back and write down the definitions.

1.

2.

3.

4.

5.

6.

7.

8.

9.

10.

KEY: SHORT ANSWER UNIT TEST #1 - *Island of the Blue Dolphins*

I. Matching/Identify

_G_ Sea Elephant tooth		A. Yellow-bearded Russian
_M_ Channel Islands		B. Wished to marry Nanko
_H_ Black Cave		C. Female tamed bird
_I_ Rontu		D. Aleut girlfriend
_A_ Captain Orlov		E. Dropped scallops from the sky
_K_ Devilfish		F. When Indians settled on island
_E_ Pelican		G. Needed for spear
_N_ Santa Barbara		H. Sea grotto with row of statues
_B_ Ulape		I. Yellow-eyed dog
_O_ Chief Chowig		J. Survived eighteen years alone
_C_ Lurai		K. Arms have rows of suckers
_D_ Tutok		L. Author
_F_ 2000 B.C.		M. Eight islands off coast of California
_L_ Karana		N. Clifornia mission
_J_ O'Dell		O. Karana's father

II. Short Answer

1. Whose true story is this novel based upon?
   It is based on The Lost Woman of San Nicholas who was found living alone in a crude house with a dog on this island eighteen years after the Indians of Ghalas-at had been rescued.

2. For what reason had the Russian and his crew come to the island?
   He came with forty men to hunt sea otter. They wish to camp on the island while they hunt.

3. What agreement of payment was reached between the Aleuts and Karana's father, Chief Chowig?
    At first the Russian offered one part for the islanders, to be paid in goods, and two parts for them. He later agreed to equal parts for each.

4. Explain the otter slaughtering process as told by Karana.
    The Aleuts speared the otters from their canoes. At dark they brought their catch in to Coral Cove and skinned and fleshed them on the beach. In the morning the beach would be strewn with carcasses, and the waves red with blood.

5. Describe the battle between the hunters and the island warriors.
    Chief Chowig blocked an Aleut hunter's path to a boat; the Chief ended up bloodied on the rocks. He arose and his warriors, with their spears raised, rushed down from the ledge. A cannon was fired from the deck of the ship killing five warriors. The Aleuts drew their knives as the spear-carrying warriors rushed upon them on the shore. Two lines surged back and forth until Captain Orlov, who had rowed to the ship, returned with more Aleuts which forced the warriors backward to the cliffs. The few who were left, continued to fight without retreat. A storm came up, the Aleuts turned and ran to the boat.

6. How does life change in Ghalas-at?
    Women had to hunt and fish now. The men resented this. Everyone mourned terribly for the dead, it an unpeaceful time.

7. What does Karana do when she realizes the ship is not returning for her brother?
    She flings herself into the sea and swims for shore, ruining her beautiful skirt of yucca fibers which she had donned for the trip.

8. Where does Ramo go alone against Karana's instructions?
    He went to the south part of the island, near the cliff, where the canoes are hidden.

9. How does Karana end the haunting village's sights and sounds?
    She burns the village down, hut by hut.

10. What makes her decide to go against the tribe's law?
    The wild dogs, who killed Ramo keep returning.

11. Why is it difficult for her to make the weapons?
    Even though she had watched her father make them, she only watched with the eye of someone who would never do it.

12. In what way do Karana's feelings change when she returns to the island?
    She was happy to be home. Everything she saw filled her with happiness.

13. Describe the house she builds.
    She chooses a rock for the back end and lines up four poles on each side, bound together with sinew and covered with broad-leafed female kelp. She has eight poles on top, bound and covered the same way.

14. How is Karana able to work at night with no sunlight?
    She catches basketfuls of sai-sai, dries them and burns them at night.

15. What warning of her father's enters Karana's mind twice while preparing her attack?
    She fears her bow will break in a time of danger because she is a woman.

16. Why doesn't Karana shoot the wild dogs who are Rontu's rivals?
    She knew the battle was between Rontu and these dogs; if she interfered they would still fight, just at another time and place, maybe one less favorable to Rontu.

17. How does Karana feel after Tutok leaves?
    She misses her and even though she hears the sounds of the island, it seems very quiet with Tutok gone.

18. In what way have Karana's feelings changed about the island animals?
    She would not kill another living thing for they had become her friends or could become her friends. She comes to believe animals and birds are like people too, though they do not talk the same or do the same things.

19. Why did Karana stop counting the moons as they passed?
    The passing of the moons had come to mean little; she began to only make marks to count the four seasons of the year.

20. What does Karana do to prepare to leave the island?
    First she goes to the spring to bath. Then she puts on her otter cape, cormorant skirt, and black stone necklace and earrings. With blue clay she makes the mark of her tribe across her nose and also makes the sign that she is unmarried. She cooks a meal for herself and Rontu-Aru and fills her three baskets. She gets her cage with two young birds, as well.

III. Essay Answers will vary. Use your own criteria.

IV. Vocabulary
    Choose ten of the vocabulary words to read orally for the vocabulary section of this unit test.

SHORT ANSWER UNIT TEST 2 *Island of the Blue Dolphins*

I. Matching/Identify

___ Ulape   A. When Indians settled on island

___ Karana   B. Yellow-eyed dog

___ Lurai   C. Female tamed bird

___ O'Dell   D. Needed for spear

___ Chief Chowig   E. Dropped scallops from the sky

___ 2000 B.C.   F. Yellow-bearded Russian

___ Pelican   G. Aleut girlfriend

___ Santa Barbara   H. Sea grotto with row of statues

___ Sea Elephant tooth   I. Wished to marry Nanko

___ Captain Orlov   J. Survived eighteen years alone

___ Black Cave   K. Arms have rows of suckers

___ Tutok   L. Karana's father

___ Devilfish   M. Eight islands off coast of California

___ Channel Islands   N. California mission

___ Rontu   O. Author

Island of the Blue Dolphins Short Answer Unit Test 2 Page 2

II. Short Answer

1. How and when was the island in this story actually discovered by white men?

2. For what reason had the Russian and his crew come to the island?

3. Why do the islanders have a two names, a secret name and a common name?

4. Describe the Island of the Blue Dolphins.

5. Why were tribesmen sent to hollow out a log in the cove and sleep beside it at night?

6. What is Karana's father doing at the end of the chapter that leads you to believe he does not trust the agreement?

7. What do his daughters and the village say weakened Chief Chowig?

8. Why did the village wait three days to bury the dead?

Island of the Blue Dolphins Short Answer Unit Test 2 Page 3

9. What is the tribe's plan, under Matasaip's leadership, if the Aleuts return?

10. How does Ulape, preparing for the voyage, indicate she is unmarried?

11. Why had Ramo missed the boat?

12. Why does Karana search for weapons that may have been left behind?

13. Why is Karana losing hope of a ship returning?

14. Why does she decide to turn back for the island?

15. Upon finding the dog she shot lying helplessly, what does she do?

16. What does Tutok leave for Karana on the rock?

17. Why do you think Karana finally shares her secret name with Tutok?

Island of the Blue Dolphins Short Answer Unit Test 2 Page 4

18. Why did Karana stop counting the moons as they passed?

19. What reaction does Karana have to the sound of the white man's language?

20. After reaching the mission, what news does Karana learn of the ship that came for her people?

Island of the Blue Dolphins Short Answer Unit Test 2 Page 5

III. Quotations: Identify the speaker and explain the significance of these quotes:

1. "The sea is smooth. I think it is a flat, blue stone without any scratches. And far away on the edge of it is a small cloud which sits on the stone."

2. "I have come in peace and wish to parley. We come to hunt sea otter. We wish to camp on your island while we are hunting."

3. "Their ways are not ours nor is their language. They are people who do not understand friendship."

4. "One string of beads for one otter pelt is not our bargain. The rest of the pelts must stay here until the chests are brought."

5. "Most of those who snared fowl and found fish in the deep water and built canoes are gone. The women, who were never asked to do more than stay at home, cook food, and make clothing, now must take the place of the men and face the dangers which abound beyond the village."

6. "I do not care if the ship never comes. Tomorrow I am going to where the canoes are hidden and bring one back to Coral Cove. We will use it to fish and go looking around the island."

7. "But first you must become a man. As it is the custom, therefore, I will have to whip you with a switch of nettles and then tie you to a red-ant hill."

Island of the Blue Dolphins Short Answer Unit Test 2 Page 6

8. "I vowed that someday I would go back and kill the wild dogs in the cave. I would kill all of them. I thought of how I would do it, but mostly I thought of Ramo, my brother."

9. "As I lay there I wondered what would happen to me if I went against the laws of our tribe which forbade the making of weapons by women. Would the four winds blow in from the four directions of the world and smother me as I made the weapons? Or would the earth tremble, as many said and bury me beneath its falling rock? Or as others said, would the sea rise over the island in a terrible flood? Would the weapons break in my hands at the moment when my life was in danger, which is what my father said?"

10. "Dolphins are animals of good omen. It made me happy to have them swimming around the canoe, now that I had friends with me I did not feel the same."

11. "I was happy to be home. Everything that I saw filled me with happiness. "

12. "I did not know how lonely I had been until I had Rontu to talk to. "

13. "I never killed another animal. This is the way I felt about the animals who had become my friends and those who were not, but in time could be. If Ulape and my father had come back and laughed, and all the others had come back and laughed, still I would have felt the same way, for animals and birds are like people too, though they do not talk the same or do the same things. Without them the earth would be an unhappy place. "

14. "Rontu, you have always liked to bark at the seagulls. Whole mornings and afternoons you have barked at them. Bark at them now for me. Rontu, oh, Rontu!"

Island of the Blue Dolphins Short Answer Unit Test 2 page 7

Vocabulary

Listen to the vocabulary words and spell them. After you have spelled all the words, go back and write down the definitions.

1.

2.

3.

4.

5.

6.

7.

8.

9.

10.

KEY: SHORT ANSWER UNIT TEST 2 *Island of the Blue Dolphins*

I. Matching/Identify

- __I__ Ulape
- __J__ Karana
- __C__ Lurai
- __O__ O'Dell
- __L__ Chief Chowig
- __A__ 2000 B.C.
- __E__ Pelican
- __N__ Santa Barbara
- __D__ Sea Elephant tooth
- __F__ Captain Orlov
- __H__ Black Cave
- __G__ Tutok
- __K__ Devilfish
- __M__ Channel Islands
- __B__ Rontu

A. When Indians settled on island
B. Yellow-eyed dog
C. Female tamed bird
D. Needed for spear
E. Dropped scallops from the sky
F. Yellow-bearded Russian
G. Aleut girlfriend
H. Sea grotto with row of statues
I. Wished to marry Nanko
J. Survived eighteen years alone
K. Arms have rows of suckers
L. Karana's father
M. Eight islands off coast of California
N. California mission
O. Author

II. Short Answer

1. How and when was the island in this story actually discovered by white men?
    In the year 1602, a Spanish explorer sighted the island as he sailed north from Mexico in search of a safe haven for treasure galleons from the Philippines. He named it La Isle de San Nicholas, after the patron saint of sailors, travelers, and merchants.

2. For what reason had the Russian and his crew come to the island?
    He came with forty men to hunt sea otter. They wish to camp on the island while they hunt.

3. Why do the islanders have a two names, a secret name and a common name?
    The secret name is their real name. If it is used by people it becomes worn out and loses it magic according to Karana.

4. Describe the Island of the Blue Dolphins.
    It is two leagues long and one league wide. If you are standing on one of the hills that rise in the middle of it, the island looks like a dolphin lying on its side with its tail pointing toward the sunrise and its nose pointing to the sunset. Its fins are the reefs and rocky ledges along the shore. The wind blows strongly and constantly causing the hills to be polished smooth and the trees to be small and twisted. The village of Ghalas-at is east of the hills on a small mesa, near Coral Cove and a good spring.

5. Why were tribesmen sent to hollow out a log in the cove and sleep beside it at night?
    They were to there to watch the Aleuts, and give alarm if Captain Orlov tried to sail off without paying for the otter skins.

6. What is Karana's father doing at the end of the chapter that leads you to believe he does not trust the agreement?
    He says nothing, but works nightly on a new spear.

7. What do his daughters and the village say weakened Chief Chowig?
    They say he should never have told the Russian his secret name.

8. Why did the village wait three days to bury the dead?
    They waited due to the storm.

9. What is the tribe's plan ,under Matasaip's leadership, if the Aleuts return?
    Since they lacked men for defense, the tribe planned to flee to the island of Santa Catalina as soon as the red-sailed ship was sighted. They would all go to the cliff on the south end and let themselves down a rope of bull kelp and leave in their canoes, which had food and water stored in them.

10. How does Ulape, preparing for the voyage, indicate she is unmarried?
    She draws a thin mark of blue clay across her nose and cheekbones.

11. Why had Ramo missed the boat?
    He had forgotten his fishing spear.

12. Why does she search for weapons that may have been left behind?
    She needs them for protection for the laws of Ghalas-at forbade the making of weapons by women.

13. Why is Karana losing hope of a ship returning?
    Many seasons had passed and the time of good weather when she thought they would have come had passed.

14. Why does she decide to turn back for the island?
    The leaks grow worse and she has at least two more days to go.

15. Upon finding the dog she shot lying helplessly, what does she do?
    She picks him up, removes the arrow point, and cleanses his wound. She leaves him water and eventually feeds him. After four days, they become friends. She names him Rontu.

16. What does Tutok leave for Karana on the rock?
    She leaves a beautiful, black stone necklace.

17. Why do you think Karana finally shares her secret name with Tutok?
    She has come to like and trust Tutok.

18. Why did Karana stop counting the moons as they passed?
    The passing of the moons had come to mean little; she began to only make marks to count the four seasons of the year.

19. What reaction does Karana have to the sound of the white man's language?
    She thinks they sound very strange and wants to laugh at them at first. Then she realizes the sound of a human voice is as sweet as no sound in the world.

20. After reaching the mission, what news does Karana learn of the ship that came for her people?
    The ship had sunk in a great storm soon after it reached the mission.

III. Quotations

IV. Vocabulary
    Choose ten of the vocabulary words to read orally for the vocabulary section of the test.

ADVANCED SHORT ANSWER UNIT TEST - *Island of the Blue Dolphins*

I. Matching

___ Ulape   A. When Indians settled on island

___ Karana   B. Yellow-eyed dog

___ Lurai   C. Female tamed bird

___ O'Dell   D. Needed for spear

___ Chief Chowig   E. Dropped scallops from the sky

___ 2000 B.C.   F. Yellow-bearded Russian

___ Pelican   G. Aleut girlfriend

___ Santa Barbara   H. Sea grotto with row of statues

___ Sea Elephant tooth   I. Wished to marry Nanko

___ Captain Orlov   J. Survived eighteen years alone

___ Black Cave   K. Arms have rows of suckers

___ Tutok   L. Karana's father

___ Devilfish   M. Eight islands off coast of California

___ Channel Islands   N. California mission

___ Rontu   O. Author

Island of the Blue Dolphins Advanced Short Answer Unit Test Page 2

II. Short Answer

1. Some of the *very* things Karana fears will happen if she makes and uses weapons, happen during the course of the book. Translate O'Dell's reasons for including them.

2. How would the story have changed if Ramo had not been killed?

3. For what reason did O'Dell use Karana's secret name throughout the novel rather than her common name of Won-a-pa-lei?

4. How could Karana ultimately save and befriend Rontu when he was the dog who killed Ramo?

5. Justify the author's decision to base this survival story on a *young woman* rather than a *young man*.

Island of the Blue Dolphins Advanced Short Answer Unit Test Page 3

6. Contrast Karana's state of mind *before* and *after* her attempted canoe trip.

7. Why is Karana puzzled when her father gives his secret name to the Russian?

8. What does Karana learn about herself through this experience? How do you think it influences her life at the Santa Barbara Mission?

Island of the Blue Dolphins Advanced Short Answer Unit Test Page 4

III. Essay

Explain Karana's statement "Now that the white man had come back, I could not think of what I would do when I went across the sea, or make a picture in my mind of the white men and what they did there, or see my people who had been gone so long. Nor, thinking of the past, of the many summers and winters and springs that had gone, could I see each of them. They were all one, a tight feeling in my breast and nothing more.

IV. Vocabulary

Listen to the vocabulary words and write them down. After you have written down all the words, write a paragraph in which you use all the words. The paragraph must in some way relate to *Island of the Blue Dolphins*.

MULTIPLE CHOICE UNIT TEST 1 - *Island of the Blue Dolphins*

I. Matching

1. Father Gonzales   A. Where cormorants roost

2. Aleuts   B. Dried fish burned for light

3. Sai-sai   C. Little Girl With Large Eyes

4. Matasaip   D. Wore bone ornaments through nose

5. Ghalas-at   E. Killed Ramo

6. Kimki   F. Girl With Long Black Hair

7. Won-a-pa-lei   G. Island to the east

8. Wild dogs   H. Mission friend of lost woman

9. Coral Cove   I. Island harbor

10. Tall Rock   J. Red star in the east

11. Santa Catalina   K. Would not return for Ramo

12. Fox Eyes   L. Island village

13. Won-a nee   M. Rontu

14. Zuma   N. Sign of mourning

15. Singed hair   O. Paddled off for far country

Island of the Blue Dolphins Multiple Choice Unit Test 1 page 2

II. Multiple Choice

1. This novel is based on the true story of
    a. The Lost Woman of San Nicholas.
    b. La Brea Woman.
    c. Ghalas-at Girl.
    d. Robin Crusett.

2. The Russian and his crew came to the island to
    a. hunt sea otter.
    b. hunt dolphins.
    c. hunt cormorants.
    d. hunt sea elephants.

3. The payment agreement decided upon between Chief Chowig and the Aleuts was
    a. one part for the natives, two parts for the Aleuts.
    b. nothing for the natives.
    c. four beads per pelt for the natives.
    d. equal parts for each party.

4. Otter slaughtering involves
    a. catching them with nets.
    b. spearing them from canoes.
    c. boiling the pelts.
    d. luring them to the shore.

5. Which event *did not* occur in the battle between the hunters and the island warriors?
    a. Chief Chowig blocked a hunter's path.
    b. Aleut ship fired a cannon from its deck.
    c. Orlov returned with more hunters.
    d. none of the above

6. The major change in Ghalas-at is
    a. women must do men's jobs.
    b. children must now hunt.
    c. men must do women's jobs.
    d. all must pray at dawn to be spared from another attack.

Island of the Blue Dolphins Multiple Choice Unit Test 1 page 3

7. When Karana realizes the ship is not returning for her brother she
    a. begs Ulape to come back with her.
    b. hops in a canoe and rows back to the island.
    c. jumps into the sea, swimming for shore.
    d. forces the ship captain to return

8. Against Karana's orders, Ramo goes to
    a. where the canoes are hidden on the south end of the island.
    b. where their father is buried.
    c. Coral Cove to watch for the returning ship.
    d. none of the above

9. To end the haunting reminder of the village people, Karana
    a. moves there to be among her ancestors.
    b. burns it down.
    c. goes to the other end of the island to live.
    d. none of the above

10. What makes her decide to go against the tribe's law?
    a. She sees no sign of the returning ship.
    b. The wild dogs, who killed Ramo keep returning.
    c. She needs something to do with her time.
    d. She decides the laws of her tribe are outdated

11. Why is it difficult for her to make the weapons?
    a. She has never made them before.
    b. Women don't do such things.
    c. She has not watched her father very carefully when he made them.
    d. All of the above

12. In what way do Karana's feelings change when she returns to the island?
    a. She was happy to be home.
    b. Everything she saw filled her with happiness.
    c. She hugs the sand.
    d. All of the above.

Island of the Blue Dolphins Multiple Choice Unit Test 1 page 4

13. Choose the one thing *not true* of the house Karana builds.
    a. The back end is a large rock.
    b. The roof is made of poles covered with seaweed.
    c. The sides are made of large rocks.
    d. None of the above

14. Karana is able to work at night with no sunlight because she
    a. burns her oil lamp.
    b. burns little dried fish.
    c. uses the embers from the day fire.
    d. works when there is a full moon.

15. Her father's warning that her bow will break in a time of danger
    a. enters her mind twice during her attack.
    b. causes her not to attack.
    c. never enters her mind.
    d. causes her to aim incorrectly.

16. Karana doesn't kill Rontu's rivals because she doesn't believe in killing anymore.
    a. true
    b. false

17. After Tutok leaves, Karana
    a. misses her company and voice.
    b. pretends she is talking with her, making things up to talk about.
    c. thinks the island sounds are very quiet.
    d. all of the above

18. Karana's feelings changed about the island animals.
    a. true
    b. false

19. What does Karana *not* do to prepare to leave the island?
    a. She marks her face with the sign of her tribe.
    b. She puts on her necklace, earrings, cape, and skirt.
    c. She fills her canoe with her things.
    d. She gathers her caged birds.

20. Father Gonzales tells Karana that the ship her people came over on
    a. was preserved in a museum in San Diego.
    b. sunk in a tidal wave right after it left her island.
    c. was sent to Africa for slave trading.
    d. sunk in a great storm shortly after it made it to the mission.

Island of the Blue Dolphins Multiple Choice Unit Test 1 page 5

III. Quotations: Identify the speaker:

A= Chief Chowig   B= Ramo   C= Tutok   D= Captain Orlov

E= Nanko   F= Karana   G= Ulape   H=Matasaip

1. "The sea is smooth. I think it is a flat, blue stone without any scratches. And far away on the edge of it is a small cloud which sits on the stone."

2. "I have come in peace and wish to parley. We come to hunt sea otter. We wish to camp on your island while we are hunting."

3. "Their ways are not ours nor is their language. They are people who do not understand friendship."

4. "In the morning when he crawls out of his tent he sits on a rock and combs until the beard shines like a cormorant's wing."

5. "She is dressed in skins just like the men, but she wears a fur cap and under the cap she has thick hair that falls to her waist."

6. "The ship does not belong to our enemies, the Aleuts. There are white men on this ship and they have come from that place where Kimki went when he left our island. The ship has come for one reason, to take us away from Ghalas-at."

7. "We cannot wait for Ramo, if we do the ship will be driven on the rocks. The ship will come back for him on another day."

8. "I do not care if the ship never comes. Tomorrow I am going to where the canoes are hidden and bring one back to Coral Cove. We will use it to fish and go looking around the island."

9. "I have thought of a name. I am Chief Tanyositlopai."

10. "Tutok. Wintscha, Wintscha. Mah-nay, Karana."

11. "Rontu, you have always liked to bark at the seagulls. Bark at them now for me, Rontu!"

12. "I never killed another animal. This is the way I felt about the animals.

Island of the Blue Dolphins Multiple Choice Unit Test 1 page 6

IV. Vocabulary (Matching)

1. Decreed	A. Narrow openings
2. Carcass	B. Dead body of animal
3. Brackish	C. Die
4. Omen	D. Ordered
5. Determination	E. Black, sticky tar or asphalt found along beaches
6. Crevices	F. Conviction
7. Perish	G. Salty
8. Gnawed	H. Long, narrow shoal
9. Ponder	I. Plant with stiff, spiky leaves
10. Stunned	J. Sign; indication
11. Rival	K. Miserable
12. Sandspit	L. Uproar
13. Yucca	M. More self-important
14. Forlorn	N. Opponent
15. Pitch	O. Chewed
16. Clamor	P. Winner
17. Vainer	Q. Shocked; dazed
18. Entangled	R. Think about
19. Victor	S. Silly
20. Giddy	T. Twisted

Unit Test - *Island of the Blue Dolphins*
Multiple Choice-Matching #2

I. Matching

1. Father Gonzales
2. Aleuts
3. Sai-sai
4. Matasaip
5. Ghalas-at
6. Kimki
7. Won-a-pa-lei
8. Wild dogs
9. Coral Cove
10. Tall Rock
11. Santa Catalina
12. Fox Eyes
13. Won-a nee
14. Zuma
15. Singed hair

A. Sign of mourning
B. Island harbor
C. Island to the east
D. Rontu
E. Wore bone ornaments through nose
F. Would not return for Ramo
G. Little Girl With Large Eyes
H. Paddled off for far country
I. Dried fish burned for light
J. Red star in the east
K. Killed Ramo
L. Mission friend of lost woman
M. Where cormorants roost
N. Girl With Long Black Hair
O. Island village

Island of the Blue Dolphins Multiple Choice Unit Test 2 page 2

II. Multiple Choice

1. The island in this story was discovered in 1602 by
    a. Father Gonzales.
    b. Sebastian Vizcaino.
    c. Christopher Columbus.
    d. Saint Nicholas.

2. The Russian and his crew came to the island to
    a. hunt sea otter.
    b. hunt dolphins.
    c. hunt cormorants.
    d. hunt sea elephants.

3. The islanders have
    a. nicknames.
    b. holiday names.
    c. gods' names.
    d. none of the above

4. The Island of the Blue Dolphins mostly resembles
    a. a mesa.
    b. a dolphin.
    c. a sea elephant.
    d. a kelp bed.

5. Tribesmen were sent to hollow out a log in the cove and sleep beside it at night because
    a. they were the most skilled.
    b. seldom do trees wash ashore.
    c. they feared Orlov's men would take the tree for themselves.
    d. they were to watch in case Orlov tried to sneak away at night.

6. At the end of the chapter, Karana's father
    a. hopes to meet the single Aleut woman.
    b. helps the Aleuts load the pelts.
    c. works nightly on a new spear.
    d. waits confidently for the Russian's payment.

Island of the Blue Dolphins Multiple Choice Unit Test 2 page 3

7. The village says Chief Chowig was weakened by
    a. the hard winter.
    b. mourning his wife's recent death.
    c. telling the Russian his secret name.

8. How many days did the storm last causing the tribe to forestall burying their dead?
    a. It lasted four days.
    b. It lasted two days.
    c. It lasted three days.
    d. none of the above

9. If the Aleuts return
    a. the village plans to flee.
    b. the men will defend the island.
    c. the tribe will hide.
    d. none of the above

10. Ulape draws a thin mark of blue clay across her nose and cheekbones to indicate
    a. she is married.
    b. she is the daughter of the chief.
    c. she is unmarried.
    d. she is in mourning.

11. Ramo missed the boat because he went back for his fishing spear.
    a. false
    b. true

12. Karana searches for weapons that may have been left behind because
    a. she needs them for protection.
    b. the laws of Ghalas-at forbid women from making weapons.
    c. she doesn't have any.
    d. all of the above

13. Karana is losing hope of the ship returning because
    a. the god of the underground appeared to her.
    b. many seasons have passed.
    c. the time of good weather has passed.
    d. both b and c

Island of the Blue Dolphins Multiple Choice Unit Test 2 page 4

14. In what way do Karana's feelings change when she returns to the island?
    a. She was happy to be home.
    b. Everything she saw filled her with happiness.
    c. She hugs the sand.
    d. All of the above.

15. Which of the following *doesn't* Karana do upon finding the lead dog she shot?
    a. She carries him to her place.
    b. She tries to heal him with a coral bush.
    c. She shoots him again with her sharpest arrow.
    d. She gives him food and water.

16. What does Tutok leave for Karana on the rock?
    a. She leaves an abalone shell necklace.
    b. She leaves a set of hair combs made from gull feathers.
    c. She leaves a black stone necklace.
    d. all of the above

17. Karana shares her secret name with Tutok the first time they exchange names.
    a. true
    b. false

18. Karana stops counting the moons as they passed because
    a. it came to mean very little to her.
    b. she had forgotten the symbol for it.
    c. they came and went so swiftly.
    d. she wanted to forget how long she had been alone.

19. Karana is at first amused by the white man's speech, but then is comforted by its sound, the sound of a human voice.
    a. true
    b. false

20. Father Gonzales tells Karana that the ship her people came over on
    a. was preserved in a museum in San Diego.
    b. sunk in a tidal wave right after it left her island.
    c. was sent to Africa for slave trading.
    d. sunk in a great storm shortly after it made it to the mission.

Island of the Blue Dolphins Multiple Choice Unit Test 2 page 5

III. Quotations: Identify the speaker:

A= Karana   B= Tutok   C= Chief Chowig   D= Matasaip
E=Nank   F=Captain Orlov   G= Ulape   H= Ramo

1. "The sea is smooth. I think it is a flat, blue stone without any scratches. And far away on the edge of it is a small cloud which sits on the stone."

2. "I have come in peace and wish to parley. We come to hunt sea otter. We wish to camp on your island while we are hunting."

3. "Their ways are not ours nor is their language. They are people who do not understand friendship."

4. "In the morning when he crawls out of his tent he sits on a rock and combs until the beard shines like a cormorant's wing."

5. "She is dressed in skins just like the men, but she wears a fur cap and under the cap she has thick hair that falls to her waist."

6. "The ship does not belong to our enemies, the Aleuts. There are white men on this ship and they have come from that place where Kimki went when he left our island. The ship has come for one reason, to take us away from Ghalas-at.

7. "We cannot wait for Ramo, if we do the ship will be driven on the rocks. The ship will come back for him on another day."

8. "I do not care if the ship never comes. Tomorrow I am going to where the canoes are hidden and bring one back to Coral Cove. We will use it to fish and go looking around the island."

9. "I have thought of a name. I am Chief Tanyositlopai."

10. "Tutok. Wintscha, Wintscha. Mah-nay, Karana."

11. "Rontu, you have always liked to bark at the seagulls. Whole mornings and afternoons you have barked at them. Bark at them now for me. Rontu, oh, Rontu!"

12. "I never killed another animal. This is the way I felt about the animals who had become my friends and those who were not, but in time could be. If Ulape and my father had come back and laughed, and all the others had come back and laughed, still I would have felt the same way.

Island of the Blue Dolphins Multiple Choice Unit Test 2 page 6

IV. Vocabulary (Matching)

1. Decreed	A. Think about
2. Carcass	B. Chewed
3. Brackish	C. Die
4. Omen	D. Ordered
5. Determination	E. Winner
6. Crevices	F. Conviction
7. Perish	G. Salty
8. Gnawed	H. Silly
9. Ponder	I. Shocked; dazed
10. Stunned	J. Opponent
11. Rival	K. More self-important
12. Sandspit	L. Uproar
13. Yucca	M. Miserable
14. Forlorn	N. Dead body of animal
15. Pitch	O. Narrow openings
16. Clamor	P. Black, sticky tar or asphalt found along beaches
17. Vainer	Q. Plant with stiff, spiky leaves
18. Entangled	R. Sign; indication
19. Victor	S. Long, narrow shoal
20. Giddy	T. Twisted

ANSWER SHEET - *Island of the Blue Dolphins*
Multiple Choice Unit Tests

I. Matching
1. ___
2. ___
3. ___
4. ___
5. ___
6. ___
7. ___
8. ___
9. ___
10. ___
11. ___
12. ___
13. ___
14. ___
15. ___

II. Multiple Choice
1. (A) (B) (C) (D)
2. (A) (B) (C) (D)
3. (A) (B) (C) (D)
4. (A) (B) (C) (D)
5. (A) (B) (C) (D)
6. (A) (B) (C) (D)
7. (A) (B) (C) (D)
8. (A) (B) (C) (D)
9. (A) (B) (C) (D)
10. (A) (B) (C) (D)
11. (A) (B) (C) (D)
12. (A) (B) (C) (D)
13. (A) (B) (C) (D)
14. (A) (B) (C) (D)
15. (A) (B) (C) (D)
16. (A) (B) (C) (D)
17. (A) (B) (C) (D)
18. (A) (B) (C) (D)
19. (A) (B) (C) (D)
20. (A) (B) (C) (D)

III. Quotes
1. (A) (B) (C) (D) (E) (F) (G) (H)
2. (A) (B) (C) (D) (E) (F) (G) (H)
3. (A) (B) (C) (D) (E) (F) (G) (H)
4. (A) (B) (C) (D) (E) (F) (G) (H)
5. (A) (B) (C) (D) (E) (F) (G) (H)
6. (A) (B) (C) (D) (E) (F) (G) (H)
7. (A) (B) (C) (D) (E) (F) (G) (H)
8. (A) (B) (C) (D) (E) (F) (G) (H)
9. (A) (B) (C) (D) (E) (F) (G) (H)
10. (A) (B) (C) (D) (E) (F) (G) (H)
11. (A) (B) (C) (D) (E) (F) (G) (H)
12. (A) (B) (C) (D) (E) (F) (G) (H)

IV. Vocabulary
1. ___
2. ___
3. ___
4. ___
5. ___
6. ___
7. ___
8. ___
9. ___
10. ___
11. ___
12. ___
13. ___
14. ___
15. ___
16. ___
17. ___
18. ___
19. ___
20. ___

ANSWER SHEET KEY - *Island of the Blue Dolphins*
Multiple Choice Unit Test 1

I. Matching
1. __H__
2. __D__
3. __B__
4. __K__
5. __L__
6. __O__
7. __F__
8. __E__
9. __I__
10. __A__
11. __G__
12. __M__
13. __C__
14. __J__
15. __N__

II. Multiple Choice
1. ( ) (B) (C) (D)
2. ( ) (B) (C) (D)
3. (A) (B) (C) ( )
4. (A) ( ) (C) (D)
5. (A) (B) (C) ( )
6. ( ) (B) (C) (D)
7. (A) (B) ( ) (D)
8. (A) (B) ( ) (D)
9. ( ) (B) (C) (D)
10. (A) (B) ( ) (D)
11. (A) ( ) (C) (D)
12. (A) (B) (C) ( )
13. (A) ( ) (C) (D)
14. (A) (B) (C) ( )
15. (A) (B) ( ) (D)
16. (A) (B) ( ) (D)
17. (A) ( ) (C) (D)
18. ( ) (B) (C) (D)
19. ( ) (B) (C) (D)
20. (A) (B) (C) ( )

III. Quotes
1. (A) ( ) (C) (D) (E) (F) (G) (H)
2. (A) (B) (C) ( ) (E) (F) (G) (H)
3. ( ) (B) (C) (D) (E) (F) (G) (H)
4. (A) (B) (C) (D) (E) (F) ( ) (H)
5. ( ) (B) (C) (D) (E) (F) (G) (H)
6. (A) (B) (C) (D) ( ) (F) (G) (H)
7. (A) (B) (C) (D) (E) (F) (G) ( )
8. (A) ( ) (C) (D) (E) (F) (G) (H)
9. (A) ( ) (C) (D) (D) (F) (G) (H)
10. (A) (B) ( ) (D) (E) (F) (G) (H)
11. (A) (B) (C) (D) (E) ( ) (G) (H)
12. (A) (B) (C) (D) (E) ( ) (G) (H)

IV. Vocabulary
1. __D__
2. __B__
3. __G__
4. __J__
5. __F__
6. __A__
7. __C__
8. __O__
9. __R__
10. __Q__
11. __N__
12. __H__
13. __I__
14. __K__
15. __E__
16. __L__
17. __M__
18. __T__
19. __P__
20. __S__

ANSWER SHEET KEY - *Island of the Blue Dolphins*
Multiple Choice Unit Test 2

I. Matching
1. L
2. E
3. I
4. F
5. O
6. H
7. N
8. K
9. B
10. M
11. C
12. D
13. G
14. J
15. A

II. Multiple Choice
1. (A) ( ) (C) (D)
2. ( ) (B) (C) (D)
3. (A) (B) (C) ( )
4. (A) ( ) (C) (D)
5. (A) (B) (C) ( )
6. (A) (B) ( ) (D)
7. (A) (B) ( ) (D)
8. (A) (B) ( ) (D)
9. ( ) (B) (C) (D)
10. (A) (B) ( ) (D)
11. ( ) (B) (C) (D)
12. (A) (B) (C) ( )
13. (A) ( ) (C) (D)
14. ( ) (B) (C) (D)
15. (A) (B) ( ) (D)
16. (A) (B) ( ) (D)
17. (A) ( ) (C) (D)
18. (A) ( ) (C) (D)
19. ( ) (B) (C) (D)
20. (A) (B) (C) ( )

III. Quotes
1. (A) (B) (C) (D) (E) (F) (G) ( )
2. (A) (B) (C) (D) (E) ( ) (G) (H)
3. (A) (B) ( ) (D) (E) (F) (G) (H)
4. (A) (B) (C) (D) (E) (F) (G) ( )
5. (A) (B) (C) (D) (E) (F) ( ) (H)
6. (A) (B) (C) (D) ( ) (F) (G) (H)
7. (A) (B) (C) ( ) (E) (F) (G) (H)
8. (A) (B) (C) (D) (E) (F) (G) ( )
9. (A) (B) (C) (D) (E) (F) (G) ( )
10. (A) ( ) (C) (D) (E) (F) (G) (H)
11. ( ) (B) (C) (D) (E) (F) (G) (H)
12. ( ) (B) (C) (D) (E) (F) (G) (H)

IV. Vocabulary
1. D
2. N
3. G
4. R
5. F
6. O
7. C
8. B
9. A
10. I
11. J
12. S
13. Q
14. M
15. P
16. L
17. K
18. T
19. E
20. H

UNIT RESOURCE MATERIALS

BULLETIN BOARD IDEAS - *Island of the Blue Dolphins*

1. Research ancient Native American wall carvings and their interpretations. Reproduce and label using an opaque projector to enlarge. Students could also draw some based on Karana's descriptions or their findings.

2. Create and illustrate a timeline for the story. Try to incorporate her use of suns and moons and season changes as units of time measurement.

3. Design murals depicting favorite scenes.

4. Illustrate travel posters for the Island of the Blue Dolphins. Different students could illustrate different aspects of the island.

5. Students could write diary entries from Karana's viewpont illustrating them with sketches. Try to use language and sentence structure as she would have. These could be for any of the adventures Karana experienced on the island.

6. Graphically contrast Karana's life on the Island of the Blue Dolphins with what you think her existence was like at the mission in California. Contrast Karana's manner of dressing with female students' clothing.

7. Invite someone in to share who is familiar with or makes Native American jewelry. If not possible, research and display pictures of Native American jewelry. Discuss importance and meaning to tribal women, including those from the novel..

8. Recreate the Island of the Blue Dolphins. Use the descriptions Karana gives in chapter two and throughout the novel. Include a legend that shows the symbols you used for your features and a scale.

9. Create a composite of the main characters, surrounding them with elements and details that illustrate each of them personally.

10. Fashion apparel out of similar materials to those Karana used; colorful feathers, yucca fibers, etc. Try to recreate skirts, belts, wreaths, sandals, capes, etc. Use whatever materials that are available that would be of a similar texture. Reread sections where she describes making these for details. Display with explanations of construction. Discuss the ease or difficulty of making these items. Include number of hours necessary to complete items.

11. Display drawings. posters, or pictures of sea animals mentioned in the novel. Include statistics and information about each one. Possible topics could be: habitat, reproduction, behavior, food, use to humans, and risk of endangerment.

12. Post illustrations of figurative language from the book.

13. Display pictures of various Native American canoes and their purposes. Identify by location and tribe.

14. Have students choose a secret name for themselves. Fold a large, unlined index card (or larger piece of index paper) so that you can staple it on bulletin board and flip it up to read the underside. Students may write their secret names on the outside, illustrating it briefly. On the underside, they may write their real names. It could be a fun activity to have students guess whose secret name matches to whom. Make a nice border out of strings of colorful beads or something that relates to Karana's appearance.

15. Karana often used legends and tales handed down to her to explain certain things. Find them in the story. Prepare illustrations to go along with the short stories or write a legend of your own explaining some event or natural occurrence and illustrate it.

EXTRA ACTIVITIES - *Island of the Blue Dolphins*

One of the difficulties in teaching a novel is that all students don't read at the same speed. One student who likes to read may take the book home and finish it in a day or two. Sometimes a few students finish the in-class assignments early. The problem, then, is finding suitable extra activities for students.

One thing that helps is to keep a little library in the classroom. For this unit on *Island of the Blue Dolphins*, you might check out from the school library other books by Scott O'Dell. A biography of the author would be interesting for some students. You may include other related books and articles about: Channel Islands, San Nicolas Island, islands, tropical climate, mesas, canyons, survival, Native Americans' customs and beliefs, baskets, California missions, Aleuts, abalone, dolphins, otters, pelicans, gulls, whales, sea elephants, devilfish, fox, starfish, cormorants, seals, feral animals (packs of wild animals), stars, earthquakes, tidal waves, sea caves (grottoes), wall carvings, caves, canoes, kelp, gender roles, omens, animal rights, etc.

Other things you may keep on hand are puzzles. We have made some relating directly to *Island of the Blue Dolphins* for you. Feel free to duplicate them.

The pages which follow contain games, puzzles and worksheets. The keys, when appropriate, immediately follow the puzzle or worksheet. There are two main groups of activities: one group for the unit; that is, generally relating to *Island of the Blue Dolphins* text, and another group of activities related strictly to *Island of the Blue Dolphins* vocabulary.

Directions for the games, puzzles and worksheets are self-explanatory. The object here is to provide you with extra materials you may use in any way you choose.

MORE ACTIVITIES - *Island of the Blue Dolphins*

1. Have students pick a favorite chapter or scene to perform on a stage. Discuss the term "monologue" for scenes with only Karana thinking or speaking aloud. Some students will love portraying the dog. You could be very brave and invite a family dog in to try to play a short part of Rontu or Rontu-Aru. (This could lead to discussion about animal actors and their training.)

2. Research the meaning of the term, Aleut. ("brother of the sea otter") Represent how the Aleuts' actions in this novel *contradict* with this meaning. Act out how better their actions could have paralleled the meaning of their name.

3. Recreate the land cave near the spring where Karana makes a home (p.89) including the ancestral wall carvings, or the sea cave, Black Cave (p. 127-129), including the row of strange figures on the ledge. They could do both explaining their differences and likenesses.

4. Develop illustrated comic strip versions of selected scenes. Cut apart, mix up, and have students exchange among themselves. Time them to see who can recreate a scene the quickest.

5. List all the foods Karana mentions that she and/or her tribe eat and the manner in which they are prepared. Research the nutritional values of these foods. Compare them to today's nationally recommended standards using the nutrition pyramid. Report findings to the class.

6. Research tidal waves and earthquakes. Reread the pages (165-170) in which Karana describes these natural disasters. Are her observations accurate compared to what you found? Construct dioramas depicting these exciting scenes.

7. List the materials Karana had to work with to fashion her tools and weapons. What available materials can you locate that are somewhat similar? Try to create some tools using the items you came up with. How do your tools compare with hers? Does purpose influence the item's construction? In what way? Label these implements according to their purpose and display.

8. Show the video version of Island of the Blue Dolphins. Compare and contrast to the book. They could then write a comparison composition using their notes.

9. Compare and contrast the climate of the Channel Islands to where your students live. They could then construct a model to illustrate the likenesses and/or differences.

10. Find the natural remedies from the novel Karana uses for healing and other uses. Distinguish their ingredients and actual healing or medicinal powers. Compare to modern medicines.

11. Research the Spanish Californian missions during this time period. Debate the pros and cons of relocating the islanders from each group's perspective.

12. Students who like board games may want to create one using information from this novel. Some students could work together as a group to complete this task. Encourage them to take a very detailed look at setting to illustrate their board and use vocabulary, characters, and plot for question cards, which could be cut out in shapes of dolphins.

13. Bring in any "fur" coats (or other animal pelt/hide apparel) class members or their relatives may have. Discuss their appearance, appeal, feel, usefulness, and durability. Become informed on current issues of animal rights' activists. Hold a debate on the pros and cons of killing animals for their pelts or hides.

14. Research ceremonies for the rites of manhood in Native American tribes and other cultures. Does Karana's description of their tribe's ritual (p.44) to Ramo compare to other tribes' traditions? Why is this different in various cultures?

15. Write an account of Karana's eventual arrival at the mission in California. Devising some sort of sign language for Karana's part, write dialogue for the scene and act it out.

16. Develop an Island of the Blue Dolphins' newspaper, including traditional columns: news, features, editorials, advertisements, obituaries, weather, comics, sports, classified, advice column, real estate, etc. Base articles on the setting, plot, and characters in the novel. Have writing staff assume island pseudonyms.

17. List gender specific behavior references from the novel. Research similar dictates in other Native American cultures, and/or any other cultures of their choice. Have things changed for women/men in Native American cultures? How about in other cultures? In what ways? Present findings to the class in some manner of their choice.

18. Research civilization's hazards to sea life. Cite specific examples of harm and damage done. List and evaluate by your standards. What can be done about these things? How can they be prevented or lessened in the future? If students feel the urge, take action.

19. Develop the theme of pet companionship. What benefits or drawbacks can exist? Have students share their personal experiences (bring in pictures to share) or even physically introduce their pets to the class, if feasible. Work with local animal shelter (or take students' pets) to make pet visits to nursing homes. Monitor participating animal vaccinations carefully

20. Have girls mark their faces like Ulape and Karana did to indicate they were unmarried. How do they feel about it? How would they feel if they were to wear these marks in public? What would be the

advantage; disadvantage to this labeling? Study up to find out what other cultures do to indicate this state. Do men mark themselves? Why or why not?

21. Read other books by Scott O'Dell. Especially applicable is *Zia*, sequel to *Island of the Blue Dolphins*. Have them report to the class, comparing his writing style, themes, settings, characters, and plots to *Island of the Blue Dolphins*. Other books reflecting various cultures: *Sing Down the Moon*, Navajos; *The Feathered Serpent*, Aztecs; *The Black Pearl*, Mexican; *The King's Fifth*; Native Americans of Mexico and S.W. United States; and *Black Star, Bright Dawn*, Eskimos.

22. Compose a list of simple questions or statements Karana might have needed to use to communicate with people at the mission. Write them on the board or on strips of paper and let students choose one.. Have students volunteer to act out through the use of gestures and signs. Other students can try to decode and match up.

23. Have a seashell collection sharing session. (say **that** 3x)

24. Read other survival stories independently and share with the class. Compare and contrast survivors' ages, locations, methods, customs, values, and states of mind to Karana's. These could be books such as *Robinson Crusoe*, or short articles from magazines like *Reader's Digest*.

25. Play audio tapes of sea and sea animal sounds for the class. Have them close their eyes and imagine co-existing with those sounds twenty-four hours a day, as Karana did on her island. They could draw or write poetry about the images these sounds evoked in them.

26. Page 50 relates Karana's experience with the chest, and its contents, left by the Russian leader of the Aleuts. Bring in a chest (or have a student do this) and fill with something your students can make (beads, etc.) that represents this novel in some way. You could have the class write questions they would like to ask Karana about her experience and place them in it. A student could portray her and draw the questions out and answer them as she/he feels Karana would have (student must have strong interpretive ability) answered them. The chest could house different things at different times throughout the reading. Be creative.

27. Invite a canoe expert (or set up a visit to an outdoor supplier) to come in to inform and demonstrate about canoes. Have students prepare by reviewing information presented in the novel about the islander's canoes (size, construction, capacity, materials, purpose, etc.) Perhaps your class could even go canoeing afterwards.

28. Karana states that, "the first thing you would notice about my island is the wind." She refers to the changing direction and intensities. Research the effect of temperature, time of day, and any other factors on the strength of the wind.

29. Demonstrate and compare fisherpupils' fishing methods with those of Karana's tribe.

30. Study constellations, including the stars Karana mentions and Indians' reliance on these everpresent guides. Who uses stars today for direction? Maybe you could visit a planetarium.

31. Baskets were very important to Karana. Learn basketweaving and demonstrate techniques for the class or invite a skilled basketweaver to come in and explain techniques.

32. Karana describes many birds from the island. Review her descriptions. Identify birds in your area and compare to those on the island.

WORD SEARCH - *Island of the Blue Dolphins*

All words in this list are associated with *Island of the Blue Dolphins*. The words are placed backwards, forward, diagonally, up and down. The clues below the word search can help you find the words.

```
R O N T U A R U W O N A N E E F I R E W I N G K
T E W A U Z N O C I P D M H C U O W O P F H M B
M A T O N T F A N O N E X U C A L X Z C A R D F
D A N T N K O J R T W T L H Z T L B E L K L M S
S O H Y O A O K H A U S A I K M I K A S I P U V
J E L N O K P K C M K N Z I C H A S C A K N T H
L V Y P A S Y A A A N V N J W A A T R E S D J T
P C K E H Y I I L E L H T O O T N U A A N D A E
T B B P X I Y T L E Z B O D E L L F H S E G V L
T M Q B A O N N L F I L W C S R B C Q V A A X F
P S N S U G F T S O A X Z L U E S A I M W I M M
G W I I I T A T G H P O L R E T S L R L Z Q P H
E A T W A K E R C G R U C M N B F D A B H W A S
S O O I U K V U A L B H A I K I R D L A A L Y M
D H N M S N X R O M I N W T S E I Y I B E R I X
C O R A L C O V E N O R T H S T A R Y U C C A Z
R I B S C D O G S M P A H S A Y N O T S E H C F
```

ALEUT	DRESS	NECKLACE	TIDALWAVE
BARBARA	FIRE	NORTHSTAR	TOOTH
BASKETS	FOXES	ODELL	TUMAIYOUIT
BLACK	FOXEYES	ORLOV	TUTOK
BLUE	GHALASAT	OTTER	ULAPE
BULLS	HAIR	PAHSAYNO	URCHINS
CANOE	KARANA	PELICAN	WING
CHANNEL	KIMKI	RAMO	WINTAI
CHEST	LURAI	RIBS	WINTSCHA
CHOWIG	MAGAT	ROCK	WONANEE
CORAL	MAHNAY	RONTU	WONAPALEI
CORALCOVE	MATASAIP	RONTUARU	XUCHAL
COWS	MICE	SAISAI	YUCCA
DEVILFISH	MONAMEE	SUNS	ZUMA
DOGS	MUKAT	TAINOR	

CROSSWORD - *Island of the Blue Dolphins*

CROSSWORD CLUES - *Island of the Blue Dolphins*

ACROSS

1. God who lived
4. Personal pronoun that can be singular or plural
5. Little Girl With Large Eyes
6. Unit of time; ___ and moons
8. Survived 18 years alone
12. Mission friend of lost woman; Father ___
13. Also
14. That one (pronoun)
15. Island harbor (2 words)
18. Look at
19. Mode of transportation
20. Yellow-eyed dog
21. Wished to marry Nanko
22. Tamed male bird
23. Female tamed bird
26. Named for patron saint of sailors
30. Sign of mourning; singed ___
32. Clever thieves; red ___
34. Where cormorants roost; Tall ___
35. Negative reply
36. Made by white men for Karana to wear to mission
37. Tar-bottomed cookers

DOWN

1. Would not return for Ramo
2. Paddled off for far country
3. Brought news of ship
4. Positive response
5. Girl With Long Black Hair
6. Dried fish burned for light
7. Star that does not move
9. Missed the ship
10. Wore bone ornaments through the nose
11. Rontu
15. Eight islands off coast of California; ___ Islands
16. Wound healing power; ___ bush
17. Ingest food
21. Karana used their purple color for dying; sea ___
22. Needed for spear; sea elephant ___
24. Every one
25. Sea cave with row of statues: ___ Cave
27. Killed Ramo; wild ___
28. Yellow-bearded Russian; Captain ___
29. Food robbers
31. Female sea elephants
32. Reduced huts to ashes
33. Opposite of west

CROSSWORD ANSWER KEY - *Island of the Blue Dolphins*

M	U	K	A	T				N		Y	O	U				
A		I				W	O	N	A	N	E	E		S	U	N	S
T		M					O		N		S		A		O		
A		K	A	R	A	N	A		K			A		I		R		F
S		I		A			A		G	O	N	Z	A	L	E	S		T	O	O
A				M		P						E		A		H		X
I	T		C	O	R	A	L	C	O	V	E		U		I		S	E	E
P		H			L		O		A		T			T		Y
		C	A	N	O	E		R	O	N	T	U		U	L	A	P	E
		N		I		A				R		R		S
T	A	I	N	O	R		L	U	R	A	I		C		A
O		E			B							H		L
O		L	A	I	S	L	E	D	E	S	A	N	N	I	C	O	L	S
T	M				A		O					N		R
H	A	I	R		C		C		G		F	O	X	E	S		L
	C		R	O	C	K	S		I			A		N	O
	E		W				D	R	E	S	S		V
		B	A	S	K	E	T	S		E		T

MATCHING QUIZ/WORKSHEET 1 - *Island of the Blue Dolphins*

___ 1. Channel Islands   A. Missed the ship
___ 2. Ghalas-at   B. Star that does not move
___ 3. Ramo   C. Rontu
___ 4. Mon-a-nee   D. Eight islands off coast of California
___ 5. Captain Orlov   E. Yellow-bearded Russian
___ 6. Santa Catalina   F. Brought news of ship
___ 7. Nanko   G. Village on island
___ 8. Fox Eyes   H. Wished to marry Nanko
___ 9. Ulape   I. Little Boy With Large Eyes
___10. Lurai   J. Arms have rows of suckers
___11. Devilfish   K. Island to the east
___12. Wild dogs   L. Killed Ramo
___13. Father Gonzales   M. Female tamed bird
___14. Baskets   N. Tar-bottomed cookers
___15. Tall Rock   O. Unit of time
___16. North Star   P. Aleuts slaughtered
___17. Coral bush   Q. Wound healing power
___18. Pelican   R. Mission friend of lost woman
___19. Otter   S. Where cormorants roost
___20. Suns and moons   T. Dropped scallops from sky

KEY: MATCHING QUIZ/WORKSHEET 1 - *Island of the Blue Dolphins*

__D__ 1. Channel Islands
__G__ 2. Ghalas-at
__A__ 3. Ramo
__I__ 4. Mon-a-nee
__E__ 5. Captain Orlov
__K__ 6. Santa Catalina
__F__ 7. Nanko
__C__ 8. Fox Eyes
__H__ 9. Ulape
__M__ 10. Lurai
__J__ 11. Devilfish
__L__ 12. Wild dogs
__R__ 13. Father Gonzales
__N__ 14. Baskets
__S__ 15. Tall Rock
__B__ 16. North Star
__Q__ 17. Coral bush
__T__ 18. Pelican
__P__ 19. Otter
__O__ 20. Suns and moons

A. Missed the ship
B. Star that does not move
C. Rontu
D. Eight islands off coast of California
E. Yellow-bearded Russian
F. Brought news of ship
G. Village on island
H. Wished to marry Nanko
I. Little Boy With Large Eyes
J. Arms have rows of suckers
K. Island to the east
L. Killed Ramo
M. Female tamed bird
N. Tar-bottomed cookers
O. Unit of time
P. Aleuts slaughtered
Q. Wound healing power
R. Mission friend of lost woman
S. Where cormorants roost
T. Dropped scallops from sky

MATCHING QUIZ/WORKSHEET 2 - *Island of the Blue Dolphins*

___ 1. Black stone necklace A. Clever thieves
___ 2. Chest B. Good omen
___ 3. Whale ribs C. Island word for pretty
___ 4. Earthquake D. Karana's pride sent to Rome
___ 5. Dolphin E. Dried fish burned for light
___ 6. Xuchal F. Sign of mourning
___ 7. Singed hair G. Needed for spear
___ 8. Pay-say-no H. Ground seashells and tobacco
___ 9. Red foxes I. Island word for goodbye
___10. Win-tai J. Male sea elephants
___12. Cormorant skirt L. California mission
___13. Bulls M. Unmarried signal
___14. Coral Cove N. Island harbor
___15. Blue Clay Mark O. Comprised fence
___16. Chief Chowig P. Author
___17. Sai-sai Q. Gift from Tutok
___18. Santa Barbara R. Full of beads and earrings
___19. Sea elephant tooth S. Destroyed canoes
___20. O'Dell T. Karana's father

KEY: MATCHING QUIZ/WORKSHEET 2 - *Island of the Blue Dolphins*

_Q_ 1. Black stone necklace   A. Clever thieves
_R_ 2. Chest   B. Good omen
_O_ 3. Whale ribs   C. Island word for pretty
_S_ 4. Earthquake   D. Karana's pride sent to Rome
_B_ 5. Dolphin   E. Dried fish burned for light
_H_ 6. Xuchal   F. Sign of mourning
_F_ 7. Singed hair   G. Needed for spear
_H_ 8. Pay-say-no   H. Ground seashells and tobacco
_A_ 9. Red foxes   I. Island word for goodbye
_C_ 10. Win-tai   J. Male sea elephants
_D_ 12. Cormorant skirt   L. California mission
_J_ 13. Bulls   M. Unmarried signal
_N_ 14. Coral Cove   N. Island harbor
_M_ 15. Blue Clay Mark   O. Comprised fence
_T_ 16. Chief Chowig   P. Author
_E_ 17. Sai-sai   Q. Gift from Tutok
_L_ 18. Santa Barbara   R. Full of beads and earrings
_G_ 19. Sea elephant tooth   S. Destroyed canoes
_P_ 20. O'Dell   T. Karana's father

JUGGLE LETTER REVIEW GAME CLUE SHEET - *Island of the Blue Dolphins*

SCRAMBLED	WORD	CLUE
OEACN	CANOE	Mode of transportation
SSTEABK	BASKETS	Pitch-bottomed cookers
RTOTE	OTTER	Aleuts slaughtered
STCEH	CHEST	Full of beads and earrings
IOHNDLP	DOLPHIN	Good omen
AAHQEETURK	EARTHQUAKE	Destroyed canoes
ISSFHART	STARFISH	Hard to pry loose from abalone shell
UATLE	ALEUT	Wore bone ornaments through nose
AILENPC	PELICAN	Dropped scallops from sky
OOAECCLRV	CORAL COVE	Island harbor
SAANNNSHLCEIDL	CHANNEL ISLANDS	Eight islands off coast of California
PLEAU	ULAPE	Wished to marry Nanko
MAZU	ZUMA	Medicine man killed by the Aleuts
AAASHLTG	GHALAS-AT	Village on island
TBBRRAAAAASN	SANTA BARBARA	California mission
RAINOT	TAINOR	Tamed male bird
NAKAAR	KARANA	Survived eighteen years alone
KEAVCLABC	BLACK CAVE	Sea cave with row of statues
STIMPAAA	MATASAIP	Would not return for Ramo
IIVHFEDLS	DEVILFISH	Arms have rows of sucker
XEESOFY	FOX EYES	Rontu
TACKORLL	TALL ROCK	Where cormorants roost
OKANN	NANKO	Brought news of ship
GIWCCOHEFIH	CHIEF CHOWIG	Karana's father
GODSDWLI	WILD DOGS	Killed Ramo
OMAR	RAMO	Killed by wild dogs
TTNNAAAAALCIS	SANTA CATALINA	Island to the east
LEODE	O'DELL	Author
RATSHRTON	NORTH STAR	Star that does not move
AEIHBRSWL	WHALE RIBS	Comprised Karana's fence

VOCABULARY RESOURCE MATERIALS

VOCABULARY WORD SEARCH - *Island of the Blue Dolphins*

All the words in this list are associated with *Island of the Blue Dolphins* with emphasis on the vocabulary words being studied in the unit. The words are placed backwards, forward, diagonally, up and down. The included words are listed below the word search.

```
P A R L E Y E X C A V A T I O N S S A C R A C X
S L B G N F J Y C H R P H B E N P Q T W D I G M
F A E Y D F A F G K A W I T H T M E Q U R U R P
G L N K L E A G U E S F T T E S R P R C N P N Y
K A A D B I G T G C M L I T C N R I L I O N C E
H W L I S S R N V O E Y C N T H T E N N S B E B
Z L D L L P Z A I S T L S O G T T A D K B H W D
W A R Y E I I J W S H N H E R Z S E N U E L S L
S G W F Z O N T F M I X R S N M R E G G R T K W
T T N G G R N G Q A D G E E I O O C C R L T S T
Y D U A E P M S R N B L D G U K L R L I U E N T
L R R N W K M T A Q R E A A A S C A A A V E D I
L M I Y T E S L P Q E O Y I S K R A B N M E L X
R A V I N E D A B R O F L U R E C U R A T O R Y
V K V S R A D D C R O M C R C C M E P B B S R C
P H N I E T H E S V X W E V O C X T R E G G P C
G P T H R Y D D I G C Q Q N L F A P S W E N I S
```

ABALONES	FAGGOT	LOBE	RIVAL
BRACKISH	FLAILING	LURE	SANDSPIT
CARCASS	FORBADE	MESA	SINEWS
CHAFING	FORLORN	NETTLES	SINGED
CIRCLET	GALLEONS	OMEN	STUNNED
CLAMOR	GIDDY	PARLEY	STUNTED
CORMORANTS	GNAWED	PERISH	TRINKETS
CREVICES	GRUEL	PITCH	VAINER
CURATOR	HEADLAND	PONDER	WARILY
DECREED	INTRUDERS	PROW	WARY
DUNE	KELP	PURSUER	WRECKAGE
ENTANGLED	LAIR	RAVINE	YUCCA
EXCAVATIONS	LEAGUES	RESTRAIN	

VOCABULARY CROSSWORD - *Island of the Blue Dolphins*

VOCABULARY CROSSWORD CLUES - *Island of the Blue Dolphins*

ACROSS

- 2 Hold back; control
- 5 Meet; hold a discussion
- 8 Steep-sided, high flat land
- 9 More self important
- 11 Negative reply
- 12 Chewed
- 14 Coarse, brown seaweed
- 16 Rounded hill of sand formed by the wind
- 18 Person in charge of a museum
- 19 Animal that meows
- 20 Large sailing vessels
- 24 Round leafy projection
- 25 Trap
- 26 Made Karana's fence; whale ___
- 27 Ingests food
- 28 Unit of time; ___ and moons
- 31 Die
- 34 Burnt; scorched
- 35 Missed the ship
- 37 Winner
- 39 Shocked; dazed
- 40 Like a sweet potato
- 41 Definite article
- 42 The rule of the land; attorney-at-___
- 43 Miserable
- 44 Dried fish burned for light

DOWN

- 1 Sign; indication
- 2 Long, deep hollow in the ground made by a stream
- 3 Loafers
- 4 Stuff we breathe
- 5 Front end; bow
- 6 Look at words and understand them
- 7 Digs
- 10 Trespassers
- 12 Think cooked cereal
- 13 Edible
- 15 Three miles unit of measurement
- 16 Ordered
- 17 Plants armed stinging hairs
- 21 Den of wild animals
- 22 Tendons
- 23 Baubles; jewels
- 29 Eight islands off coast of California; ___ Islands
- 31 Think about
- 32 Opponent
- 33 Cautious
- 36 Paddled off for far country
- 38 Female sea elephants

VOCABULARY CROSSWORD ANSWER KEY - *Island of the Blue Dolphins*

VOCABULARY WORKSHEET 1 - *Island of the Blue Dolphins*

_____ 1. Wreckage   A. Front part; bow

_____ 2. Reproachfully   B. Cautiously

_____ 3. Vanquished   C. Thrashing

_____ 4. Victor   D. Excess

_____ 5. Prow   E. Miserable

_____ 6. Circlet   F. Three mile measurement

_____ 7. Giddy   G. Twisted

_____ 8. Flailing   H. With disapproval

_____ 9. Entangled   I. Black, sticky tar or asphalt found on beaches

_____ 10. Singed   J. Hold back

_____ 11. Warily   K. Ordered

_____ 12. Decreed   L. Ring-shaped ornament

_____ 13. Ponder   M. Think about

_____ 14. Pitch   N. Opponent

_____ 15. Forlorn   O. Ruins

_____ 16. Rival   P. Silly

_____ 17. Leagues   Q. Sleepy; lazy

_____ 18. Parley   R. Trespassers

_____ 19. Intruders   S. Burnt; scorched

_____ 20. Restrain   T. Cautiously

KEY: VOCABULARY WORKSHEET 1 - *Island of the Blue Dolphins*

__O__ 1. Wreckage		A. Front part; bow
__H__ 2. Reproachfully		B. Cautiously
__D__ 3. Vanquished		C. Thrashing
__T__ 4. Victor		D. Defeated
__A__ 5. Prow		E. Miserable
__L__ 6. Circlet		F. Three mile measurement
__P__ 7. Giddy		G. Twisted
__C__ 8. Flailing		H. With disapproval
__G__ 9. Entangled		I. Black, sticky tar or asphalt found on beaches
__S__ 10. Singed		J. Hold back
__B__ 11. Warily		K. Ordered
__K__ 12. Decreed		L. Ring-shaped ornament
__M__ 13. Ponder		M. Think about
__I__ 14. Pitch		N. Opponent
__E__ 15. Forlorn		O. Ruins
__N__ 16. Rival		P. Silly
__F__ 17. Leagues		Q. Meet; hold a discussion
__Q__ 18. Parley		R. Trespassers
__R__ 19. Intruders		S. Burnt; scorched
__J__ 20. Restrain		T. Winner

VOCABULARY WORKSHEET 2 - *Island of the Blue Dolphins*

___ 1. Chafing		A. Uproar
___ 2. Gruel		B. Conviction
___ 3. Abalones		C. Seaweed
___ 4. Sinews		D. Shoal extending from shore
___ 5. Crevices		E. Die
___ 6. Clamor		F. Rubbing
___ 7. Determination		G. Plant with stiff pointy leaves
___ 8. Sandspit		H. Thin, cooked cereal
___ 9. Trinkets		I. Edible shellfish with mother-of-pearl shell
___ 10. Nettles		J. Tendons
___ 11. Ravine		K. Narrow openings
___ 12. Gnawed		L. Plants armed with stinging hairs
___ 13. Lair		M. Chewed
___ 14. Omen		N. Bundle of sticks used for fuel
___ 15. Brackish		O. Baubles; jewelry
___ 16. Faggot		P. Deep hollow in ground
___ 17. Mesa		Q. Salty
___ 18. Yucca		R. Steep-sided high flatland
___ 19. Kelp		S. Den of wild animals
___ 20. Perish		T. Sign; indication

KEY: VOCABULARY WORKSHEET 2 - *Island of the Blue Dolphins*

F	1. Chafing	A. Uproar
H	2. Gruel	B. Conviction
I	3. Abalones	C. Seaweed
J	4. Sinews	D. Shoal extending from shore
K	5. Crevices	E. Die
A	6. Clamor	F. Rubbing
B	7. Determination	G. Plant with stiff pointy leaves
D	8. Sandspit	H. Thin, cooked cereal
O	9. Trinkets	I. Edible shellfish with mother-of-pearl shell
L	10. Nettles	J. Tendons
P	11. Ravine	K. Narrow openings
M	12. Gnawed	L. Plants armed with stinging hairs
S	13. Lair	M. Chewed
T	14. Omen	N. Bundle of sticks used for fuel
Q	15. Brackish	O. Baubles; jewelry
N	16. Faggot	P. Deep hollow in ground
R	17. Mesa	Q. Salty
G	18. Yucca	R. Steep-sided high flatland
C	19. Kelp	S. Den of wild animals
E	20. Perish	T. Sign; indication

VOCABULARY JUGGLE LETTER REVIEW GAME CLUES - *Island of the Blue Dolphins*

SCRAMBLED	WORD	CLUE
AIPDSSNT	Sandspit	Narrow shoal extending from shore
OEABRFO	Forbade	Outlawed
HKAIRBCS	Brackish	Salty
NWIESS	Sinews	Tendons
RMLCAO	Clamor	Uproar
RAWY	Wary	Cautious
ONSBLAAE	Abalones	Edible shellfish
EONM	Omen	Sign; indication
DGWNAE	Gnawed	Chewed
IHPCT	Pitch	Black, sticky tar found on beach
TTDSUNE	Stunted	Shortened
RRCOAUT	Curator	Person in charge of a museum
SAELOLGN	Galleons	Large sailing vessels
VERANI	Ravine	Deep hollow made by stream
SREIHP	Perish	Die
EEUASGL	Leagues	Three miles unit of measurement
EDDCERE	Decreed	Ordered
EGULR	Gruel	Thin, cooked cereal
DNORPE	Ponder	Think about
IEASRTN	Restrain	Hold back
PEKL	Kelp	Seaweed
AASRSCC	Carcass	Dead body of an animal
SCEERVCI	Crevices	Narrow openings
FIAGCNH	Chafing	Rubbing
UNED	Dune	Rounded hill of sand
LARIV	Rival	Opponent
CYCUA	Yucca	Plant with stiff, pointy leaves
UURREPS	Pursuer	Hunter, tracker
DDAAEHLN	Headland	High point of land extending into sea
LRAEYP	Parley	Meet; hold a discussion
SEAM	Mesa	Steep-sided high flat land
OORRMNTASC	Cormorants	Large, web-footed sea birds
EEWRKCAG	Wreckage	Ruins
DYDIG	Giddy	Silly